D1328218

Leisure and the
Rise of the Public Library

Leisure and the
Rise of the Public Library

Robert Snape

LIBRARY ASSOCIATION PUBLISHING
LONDON

Published by
Library Association Publishing
7 Ridgmount Street
London WC1E 7AE

First published 1995

British Library Cataloguing in Publication Data
A catalogue record for this book is available from the British Library

ISBN 1-85604-131-X

Typeset from author's disk in 10/13pt Palermo by Library Association Publishing
Printed and made in Great Britain by Bookcraft (Bath) Ltd

Contents

Acknowledgements

====

I would like to record my thanks to Dr. John Langrish and Mr. Jim Turner of the Institute of Advanced Studies of the Manchester Metropolitan University and to Dr. Gill Burrington for their guidance and advice throughout the research for my doctoral thesis upon which this book is largely based. I would also like to thank the librarians of the Blackburn, Darwen and Wigan reference libraries for easing access to documentary sources.

Finally I would like to thank my family for their patience and support.

Chapter 1

Leisure and Public Libraries

INTRODUCTION

Public libraries seem always to have had an ambivalent relationship with leisure. Leisure and recreation have been major reasons for the public's use of libraries since they were introduced in the middle of the nineteenth century, and libraries are now visited for leisure purposes by millions of people each year; in 1990–1, over 300 million adult fiction books were borrowed from public libraries in the United Kingdom, representing 71% of all adult books issued.[1] Reading fiction is a major leisure activity, and although adult fiction does not constitute the largest segment of publishing output in terms of titles produced, it is easily the most profitable in terms of revenue, being in itself a multi-million pound industry. Public libraries buy more adult fiction than any other category of book, and the writers whose books are borrowed the most frequently are almost without exception the major popular novelists – at the time of writing, they include Catherine Cookson, Len Deighton, Stephen King and Ruth Rendell. Most recently, the Department of National Heritage's review of the public library service has shown that borrowers read mainly for pleasure, and that many users value the library as a place for meeting friends or for relaxing.[2] In addition to books, records, tapes and compact discs are borrowed for leisure listening, and the reading of informal magazines in the library itself is another example of leisure use. Many urban libraries have a further leisure dimension through possessing facilities for presenting exhibitions, concerts and recitals. It is important too to realize that many books classified in statistics of loans as non-fiction are in fact borrowed either for leisure reading, such as biographies, humorous books and books on the royal family, or as an adjunct to other leisure interests; for example, books about hobbies, sports and holidays. It is adult fiction, however, which forms the largest single category of books borrowed from public libraries, and many readers depend solely upon libraries for newly published hardback novels; indeed, were it not for library purchases of hardback fiction, it is probable that much novel publishing would cease to be commercially viable. On this evidence, it would seem reasonable to consider public libraries to be major providers of leisure, but the fact remains that many librarians dislike the dominance of popular fiction and the concept of the public library as a leisure institution.[3]

There are several reasons for this, principally the complex nature of the service provided by libraries which incorporates information and education in addition to leisure. Public libraries have many functions, among which the provision of information to individuals, communities and businesses is an important service, with wide-ranging social and economic benefits. They also have an essential educational role and offer support to students of all ages and educational levels. Librarians have historically been more interested in the education and information functions of the public library. During the last century, the ideal of the public library as a source of educational and enlightening books for working-class men was a prevailing inspirational theme of the professional literature, and the Public Libraries Act of 1919 and the subsequent development of county libraries reinforced the association of libraries with education. In the inter-war years, there was interest in the development of commercial and technical libraries and library services to schools, and although there was some initial sociological exploration of reading habits and library use, this did not evolve into a major area of research.[4] In the post-war decades, the emphasis on information and education became more pronounced and several innovative projects were undertaken in the provision of information services to business and industry. Most of the major developments of the past 20 years have been in reference services, community information and computerized information retrieval, while the leisure function of libraries has received a fairly low priority in comparison.

The structure of local government has also contributed to antipathy between libraries and leisure. Public libraries have never had a consistent position within the local authority structure and, before 1974, although some were in autonomous departments, many were linked to education, museums or arts, or were situated in generalized conglomerates. The reorganization of 1974 placed many library services within the then newly formed leisure departments, and some senior librarians lost ultimate control of the library service to a leisure director. A degree of resentment to the provision of libraries within leisure departments accordingly formed. The fear that a 'free' public library service might be endangered if it were too overtly leisure-orientated is sometimes cited as a further reason that libraries should not be in leisure departments.[5] Finally, the training and education of librarians focuses on computerized information retrieval and information management, and leisure-related topics such as libraries and the arts, or popular fiction and its readership, have been curtailed or marginalized to accommodate this.

Affirmations of the library's leisure functions

Nevertheless, leisure has been recognized as an integral function of the public library by several writers, and indeed in many official documents. In 1927, the Kenyon Report expressed a view of the leisure function of public libraries that would not be shared by some librarians even today, when it stated that a major aim of the public library was the relief of 'the tedium of idle hours quite irrespective of intellectual profit or educational gain' and that it was sufficient if the borrower was 'rendered a happier (and not necessarily a more learned) man' by his use of the library.[6] In a similar vein, Lionel McColvin, the most influential librarian of the inter-war years, said that libraries should serve all and any activities of their readers, and that the provision of recreational 'pastime" reading was a fully valid public library function.[7] More recently, the Public Libraries Research Group has published a statement of the aims and objectives of public libraries in which leisure has a central role, particularly in the library's provision of books and other items for relaxation.[8] Perhaps more significantly in terms of library practice, the Public Libraries Act of 1964 did not restrict libraries' objectives to education or information provision but clearly stated that they had a recreational role, and although very few library services are now operated through education departments, a great many are located within leisure directorates, and thus share leisure-based objectives and policies with leisure centres, parks, museums and other types of leisure facilities and services.[9] Whatever their position in the local authority structure, all public libraries provide considerable stocks of fiction which are borrowed in large numbers, and leisure is a significant factor in their popularity. It has in fact been suggested that leisure is almost the only function of many libraries, as library authorities spend, on a rough average, 60% of their total budget on leisure services.[10] Yet, with only a few exceptions, there has been a relatively small number of publications dealing specifically with the leisure function of public libraries or with the marketing of libraries in a leisure context.[11]

The Great Fiction Question

Debate of the leisure function of public libraries is not a recent phenomenon. Leisure has raised problematic questions for public libraries since they were founded, most obviously in the area of the provision of popular fiction, but in other aspects too, such as the provision of smoking and games rooms, the blacking out of betting information in newspapers, the imposition of silence in rooms which readers were supposedly using for recreational purposes and the effects leisure was perceived to have on the professional image and status of librarians.[12] When public libraries were introduced, it was hoped by many of their supporters that they would provide working-class readers with a means of self-education and improvement. Libraries were notably successful in this, and provided technical knowledge and opportunities for personal development through their provision of educational books and journals. However, most people used them primarily for borrowing 'free' recreational reading, mainly popular fiction, and, in quantitative terms, this quickly became the dominant element in public library use. Before the turn of the century it was not uncommon for adult fiction to constitute 80% of a public library's total issue, and in only a small number of libraries did fiction account for less than half the issue. This was a matter of concern to all but a small minority of librarians, and much effort was invested in attempting to change this pattern of use, not least because it provided the numerous critics of libraries with an easy line of attack. Indeed, resentment to the public library as an institution which provided novels 'on the rates' was often sufficiently powerful to prevent the adoption of the Libraries Acts, such as occurred in Accrington in 1887.[13]

The 'Great Fiction Question', as the debate upon the provision of fiction in public libraries came to be known, was in fact not one question but two: should public libraries provide fiction and, if so, what type and standard of fiction? This was the single most controversial issue in public library development before the First World War, and split the library profession into three broad groups: those who wished to ban fiction from libraries altogether, those who felt only a restricted range of literary fiction should be stocked, and a third group who were more open-minded and felt fiction should be provided if the public wanted it. There has always been some degree of animosity to fiction among librarians and, although this may not be as widespread as it once was, it is not extinct.[14] In the recent past, fiction purchases have been disproportionately cut or suspended when book funds have been under pressure, and some libraries have implemented a policy of not buying Mills and Boon romances; Preston library, for example, refused on principle until 1980 to buy titles from this publisher.

The use of public libraries for leisure is well established, and the provision of assistance to make a 'positive use of leisure time' has recently been affirmed as a public library objective by the Library and Information Services Council.[15] The importance of leisure to public libraries is likely to increase rather than diminish, for as working patterns change and leisure time increases, the need and demand for leisure opportunities and facilities will become more urgent, a point also noted by the Department of National Heritage review. Furthermore, the introduction of competitive tendering or some other form of private sector involvement in the public library service may be implemented in leisure-related areas, and the provision of adult fiction would present an attractive commercial opportunity to the private sector as even a modest charge would generate a large income. The paradox of fiction provision in libraries is that popular fiction remains the most effective means of encouraging library use, and issue statistics, although widely disliked as a measurement of a library's work, have nevertheless been confirmed by the Audit Commission as a major performance indicator.[16] The Citizens' Charter too identifies the number of books issued and the number of visits to libraries as measures of performance, and these are clearly related to the library's leisure appeal. It is also worth recording that leisure professionals consider public libraries to be an integral element of local authority leisure provision; a recent statement[17] issued by the Institute of Leisure and Amenity Management on behalf of the Museums Association, the Tourism Society, the Chief Leisure Officers Association and other organisations with an interest in leisure, highlighted the role of libraries, museums and sport and recreation facilities in promoting a constructive use of leisure time.

Most general histories of public libraries deal in passing with the Great Fiction Question without offering a critical analysis of its significance, nor of that of the role of leisure in public library development.[18] The ways in which public libraries handled fiction were markedly influenced by the growth of the readership for popular fiction and by the cultural and social importance of English literature and the English novel. Although literary merit is now rarely a criterion in the selection of fiction, it was important in the nineteenth century, and the distinctions between 'high' and 'low' literature were crucial factors in book selection. If public library development is assessed in this context, the arguments about which types of fiction should be provided, the methods by which fiction was selected and the provision of guidance and advice to readers in choosing fiction acquire a deeper cultural significance, and enable library practice to be evaluated in a wider social and political framework.

The relevance of the past to the present

This book deals primarily with the years between 1850, the year of the first Public Libraries Act, and 1914, which, in addition to marking the outbreak of the First World War, was also the year preceding the publication of the Adams Report,[19] which heralded the Public Libraries Act of 1919, the birth of county libraries, and a new phase in public library development. At this point, it is reasonable to ask why fiction provision in public libraries 100 years ago should be considered significant to today's service. It is relevant because the 'fiction question' was not satisfactorily concluded and consequently the library profession never rationalized its position in terms of leisure. Many of the unresolved aspects of the fiction question are found in the current debates about the provision of fiction, the leisure function of libraries, professional autonomy and stock selection, and the rationale for public sector leisure provision in general. Several controversial features of fiction provision in the period up to the First World War have again come to the fore: subscription departments, interference in operational matters by library committees for political or social ends, the need to react to public demand and the reduction of spending on fiction to finance other elements of the service, were all points of debate and discussion in the period covered by this book. Many groups have an interest in the present and future development of public libraries – librarians, leisure directors and managers, undergraduates entering these professions, councillors and, of course, the users of public libraries – and it is to these that this book will primarily appeal. However, the evolution of the Great Fiction Question is also a revealing facet of social history and the general reader should not find what follows of a too narrow professional interest nor of a too technical nature.

LEISURE AND RECREATION IN THE PUBLIC LIBRARY CONTEXT

The word 'leisure' is widely used in the context of the public library service – libraries provide 'leisure' and are often part of 'leisure' departments, but what does this mean? There is no universally accepted definition of leisure and it is important to realize that, although leisure is now a commonly used word, it is rarely found in the period in which public libraries were introduced, for the Victorians preferred 'recreation'. This is a significant distinction.

Leisure

'Leisure' is derived from the Latin *licere*, and embodies concepts of choice and freedom. Leisure theorists have argued about whether leisure is best thought of as time or activity, but the key point is that leisure essentially embraces the freedom to choose. In this sense, virtually any activity can be a leisure activity, for one individual's leisure may be another's work; one reader's choice of book for leisure reading may not be that of another. Circumstances too will dictate leisure choices – most of us will at some stage have rejected a novel which we will have read with enjoyment at a later stage in life. What endows an activity with leisure quality is difficult to state precisely, but elements of freedom of choice and enjoyment are clearly important. One of the more concise modern definitions of leisure states that leisure is simply 'relatively freely undertaken non-work activity',[20] which, although a loose and qualified definition, serves well in most current instances, and reflects the common usage of the word; reading novels and magazines and using public libraries would both be included within such a definition.

Leisure serves a number of functions. It provides physical and mental rest and recuperation, and offers relief from boredom. Many leisure activities promote these ends, including the reading of any type of novel which appeals to the reader. Charles Dickens, Edgar Allan Poe, Iris Murdoch, Jilly Cooper, Stephen King, Catherine Cookson, Jeffery Archer, Mills and Boon authors and all other writers of fiction, irrespective of intrinsic or literary merit, provide individual readers with relaxation and entertainment. Leisure also offers opportunities for personal development and, again, fiction can enable readers to widen their knowledge and to gain a deeper understanding of human nature, though there would doubtless be arguments as to whether some novels had the potential to do so. It is probably with the personal development aspect of leisure that libraries generally feel most comfortable, as it embraces forms of informal education as well as the use of the library to obtain information to support other leisure activities. A further benefit of leisure is its encouragement of socialization and meeting other people. In some instances, this aspect may be the most important and, while reading may at first appear to be a highly individual pursuit, many fiction readers like to discuss their favourite authors with other readers, and for older citizens a visit to the library to borrow novels in the company of friends can be a much valued social activity – perhaps the only opportunity of the day to talk to someone else. Additionally, the books pages in newspapers and book programmes on television and radio provide novel-readers with a sense of belonging to a reading community.

Leisure also has a social dimension which differs according to place and historical period; in Greek civilization, for example, leisure was central to the idea of a good and proper life, but was largely confined to wealthy citizens and denied to slaves. In the industrialized societies of the past two centuries, leisure has become a core element in society to which all have a right; it is a major arena of commercial enterprise and of public sector provision. Leisure cannot be isolated from other aspects of society, and, as the French sociologist Joffre Dumazedier has stated, leisure is a 'product' of industrialization,[21] meaning that leisure is influenced and shaped by other social factors such as work, politics and cultural and religious values. Leisure is thus not free in an absolute sense, but is shaped and regulated by social and cultural norms. Sometimes this influence is fairly obvious, as, for example, in the way in which time for leisure is determined by the amount of time taken by work, or in enforced restrictions such as the censoring of books and films, the banning of dog fighting and the suppression of the use of certain drugs. In other instances, distinctions are more subtle, and cultural norms, class structure and media representation all contribute to the creation of a hierarchy of leisure activity. This too can be clearly observed in fiction, where the standards of what is socially acceptable and culturally valuable are not absolute, but change as society changes, as, for example, with novels which would have been considered too sexually explicit to be sold in bookshops or stocked by public libraries 30 years ago, but which are now commonly found in both outlets. These distinctions have impinged upon fiction provision in public libraries, where genre and other popular fiction read simply for amusement and relaxation has been valued less than literary or middle-brow fiction. This was particularly so in the nineteenth century, when fiction and its reading were continuously debated and discussed within the context of Victorian concepts of recreational activity.

Recreation

Recreation is a less complex word, derived from the latin *recreatio*, meaning to restore health or to renew. Recreation is narrower in meaning than leisure, for, while all recreation is a form of leisure, not all leisure is necessarily recreation. In the Victorian era, the idea of recreation embodied virtues of self-improvement and utility, and recreational activity, including popular reading, was expected to fulfil some positive purpose and not to be undertaken simply for relaxation or idle amusement. Recreation was meant to be purposeful, systematic and to have the capacity to render some improving effect, physical or mental, on the individual. To serve such a function, recreation had to be directed and there were many groups who, for political, religious, moral or economic purposes, took an active interest in its promotion. One observer, writing in 1879, reflected a widely held contemporary view in stating that recreation should be not a pastime undertaken merely for pleasure, but 'an act of duty undertaken for the sake of the subsequent power which it generates and the subsequent profit which it insures'; he also thought that public institutions of all kinds had a duty to provide recreation in the interests of 'national health, happiness, morals, and intelligence'.[22] His view had important implications for public libraries, for librarians too were interested in the potential of recreation to restore and to improve; in a speech delivered at the Library Association's meeting in 1881, Richard Garnett, the Superintendent of the British Museum Reading Room, portrayed public libraries as a means of innocent recreation and an influence for good among the mass of the people.[23] Recreative reading was meant to effect some positive outcome in the reader, either in the form of providing knowledge and information in a digestible way or in promoting morality, temperance and other social values. While some novels were written specifically with these aims, others were written simply to excite, thrill, or shock, and were subsequently disliked by critics and librarians.

A LEISURE STUDIES APPROACH TO PUBLIC LIBRARY DEVELOPMENT

Historians agree that public libraries were not introduced because of one single factor, but were hybrid institutions born of mixed motives of spreading technical education, promoting literacy and providing an improving form of recreation. Most histories of public library development have been written from the perspective of the library profession, and have emphasized the educational motives for libraries,[24, 25] and, although some more recent accounts do acknowledge the role of the public library in providing what was seen to be a better recreational resource than the public house, only Paul Sykes' book *The public library in perspective*[26] seriously considers the significance of leisure to public library development. Conversely, several historians of leisure have identified public libraries as major elements in the leisure reforms of the nineteenth century: Haywood,[27] Golby and Purdue,[28] Cunningham[29] and Bailey[30] all refer to public libraries as a response to the need to provide better leisure facilities and opportunities in the mid-nineteenth century. To approach library history from the leisure studies angle allows library development to be examined from two different and interesting perspectives. The first of these investigates the introduction of public libraries not with reference to education and technical knowledge but to the reform of leisure in the mid-nineteenth century, and considers how public libraries were seen as one means to provide better recreational opportunities for working-class people. To examine public library development from this viewpoint is not to suggest that educational motives were unimportant in the introduction of public libraries, but simply to recognize that education was not the sole factor in their introduction. This involves an evaluation, provided in the following chapter, of the complex reasoning which resulted in the first Public Libraries Act and helps to explain why public libraries today have an impossibly wide range of objectives.

The second perspective focuses on the leisure uses of public libraries once they were established, mainly because in the formative years of public libraries reading fiction was a major leisure activity and was accordingly a widely discussed social topic. The controversies surrounding the provision of popular fiction in public libraries were only one aspect of a much wider concern about what people read and indeed about popular leisure in general, and therefore an examination of the ways in which libraries provided or regulated popular fiction is in essence an investigation of the relationships between public library practice and the cultural values, literary standards and social ideals of the period. This reveals a further interesting aspect of public libraries, for, as will be explained in Chapter 2, there was much interest in the nineteenth century in exploring ways in which leisure could be manipulated to promote class harmony; indeed, one writer has gone so far as to suggest that the early campaigners for public libraries, who were 'consciously seeking to shape the taste and habits of the working class',[31] were in fact attempting to achieve a degree of social control through public libraries. This assertion may at first seem of little relevance to today's public libraries, but it is not too difficult to draw some comparisons with pressure groups which campaign for libraries to stock fiction which embodies certain values or promotes particular images. It is also important to realize that nineteenth-century libraries reflected the nature of the councils which operated them, just as library services today reflect local priorities and council policies, and that local practice in fiction provision reflected the political and social structure of the community served by the library.

In the nineteenth century, the use of libraries for 'purposeful' or 'improving' leisure, such as personal development or reading serious fiction, was generally greeted with approval, mainly because this could be argued to be essentially educational. For example, the library campaigner Thomas Greenwood proposed that Walter Scott's novels should be classed as history and those of Dickens and Thackeray as moral philosophy.[32] The function of leisure in promoting simple relaxation and entertainment was not highly valued by the library profession before the First World War, and though today library shelves bear testimony to a more relaxed approach to popular and genre fiction, there is a residual disagreement within the profession as to whether this is a valid purpose.

The impossibility of absolute freedom in leisure and the related necessity to impose some sanctions and constraints combine to make leisure a most revealing aspect of society. While few people would disagree that leisure activities likely to cause personal injury to non-participants or damage to property should not be allowed, there would be sharp differences of opinion as to whether a government or institution was entitled to restrict or license leisure beyond necessary limits. To understand a society properly it is essential to understand its attitudes to leisure – what is allowed or prohibited, encouraged or discouraged, enjoyed by all social classes groups or limited to certain classes. This could be applied to public libraries, for no other aspect of the service exposes more clearly the relationships between libraries and their social and cultural environment or accounts for the evolution of the concept of the librarian as a reader's guide or adviser.

NOTES AND REFERENCES TO CHAPTER 1

1   CIPFA, *Public library statistics*, 1990–91 (Actuals).
2   Department of National Heritage, *Review of the public library service in England and Wales*, Aslib, 1994.

3   A notable exception to this dominant view appears in Paul Sykes' book *The public library in perspective: an examination of its origins and modern role*, Bingley, 1979.

4   See: Kelly, T., *A history of public libraries in Great Britain 1845–1975*, Library Association, 1977, Chapter 11.

5   Colehan, P., 'Keep libraries out of leisure', *Assistant librarian*, May 1988, 74–6.

6   Great Britain, Board of Education, *Report on public libraries in England and Wales*, Cmnd. 2868, HMSO, 1927, paras. 284–5.

7   McColvin, L., *The public library system of Great Britain*, Library Association, 1942, 2–5.

8   *Public library aims and objectives*, Public Libraries Research Group, 1981.

9   For details of the position of public library services in specific local authorities, see: *The libraries directory 1991–93*, James Clarke, 1992.

10   Lovell, G., 'The leisure services context', *Library review*, **33** (1), Spring 1984, 14–21.

11   See for example: Kinnell, M., and MacDougall, J., *Meeting the marketing challenge: marketing strategies for public libraries and leisure services*, Taylor Graham, 1994, and Van Riel, R., 'The case for fiction', *Public library journal*, **8** (3), 1993, 81–4.

12   Snape. R., 'Betting, billiards and smoking: leisure in public libraries', *Leisure studies*, **11**, 1992, 187–99.

13   *Accrington Observer*, 26 March 1887.

14   See: Dixon, J. (ed.), *Fiction in libraries*, Library Association Publishing, 1986, 9.

15   Library and Information Services Council, *Setting objectives for public library services: a manual of public library objectives*, HMSO, 1991.

16   *Library Association record*, February 1993, 66.

17   Institute of Leisure and Amenity Management, *Statement by bodies representing those providing local authority leisure services in Great Britain*, May 1993.

18   See: Sturges, P. and Barr, A., 'The fiction nuisance in nineteenth century British public libraries', *Journal of librarianship and information science*, **24** (1), March 1992, 23–32, for one of the few recent articles on this topic.

19   Adams, W. G. S., *A report on library provision and policy to the Carnegie United Kingdom Trustees*, CUKT, 1915.

20   Roberts, K., *Contemporary society and the growth of leisure*, Longman, 1978.

21   Dumazedier, J., *Towards a society of leisure*, Collier Macmillan, 1967.

22   Romanes, G. C. 'Recreation', *Nineteenth century*, September 1879, 401–24.

23   *Transactions and proceedings of the 4th annual meeting of the Library Association of the United Kingdom*, 1881.

24   Minto, J., *A history of the public library movement in Great Britain*, Allen & Unwin, 1932.
25   Munford, W. A., *Penny rate: aspects of British public library history 1850–1950*, Library Association, 1951.
26   Sykes, op. cit., ref. 3.
27   Haywood, L., *Understanding leisure*, Stanley Thornes, 1990, 212–13.
28   Golby, J. M. and Purdue, A. W., *The civilization of the crowd: popular culture in England 1750–1900*, Batsford, 1984, 130–2; 147.
29   Cunningham, H., *Leisure in the industrial revolution c.1780–c.1880*, Croom Helm, 1980.
30   Bailey, P., *Leisure and class in Victorian England: rational recreation and the contest for control 1830–1885*, Routledge and Kegan Paul, 1978.
31   Thompson, F. M. L., 'Social control in Victorian Britain', *Economic history review*, Second series, **34** (2), May 1981, 189–208.
32   Greenwood, T., *Public libraries*, Cassell, 4th edn, 1894, 34.

Chapter 2
The Problem of Leisure

You don't ask no-one to bet with you. They does as they likes.

Does as they likes! No-one does that nowadays. There's a temperance party, a purity party, and a hanti-gambling party, and what they're all working for is just to stop folks from doing as they like.

George Moore Esther Waters

LEISURE AS A SOCIAL PROBLEM IN THE NINETEENTH CENTURY

The origins of the Public Libraries Act 1850 are often attributed directly to the Parliamentary Select Committee of 1849 which preceded it, yet they can be traced back much further than this. The introduction of rate-supported public libraries was not a short-term outcome of the 1849 Select Committee's recommendations, but the result of a long and complex process in which a concern about popular leisure in general and about recreational reading in particular was a major factor. There were several types of publicly available libraries before rate-supported libraries such as parish libraries, travelling libraries and subscription libraries, and all these, although not public in the modern sense of being freely available to everyone, provided a basic model of a library which could be used by sections of the general public. Mechanics' Institutes too offered a prototype in that their libraries were available to fee-paying members, and many public libraries were based upon defunct Mechanics' Institute libraries. The fact that several public libraries evolved from Mechanics' Institutes has contributed to a widespread belief that they were introduced solely for educational purposes and were used principally for obtaining technical and scientific books, but this was not so.

Leisure was at the centre of many of the social problems of the nineteenth century, and its reform was a major influence not only upon the introduction of public libraries but upon their mode of operation once they were established. However, to say that leisure was a social problem in the nineteenth century raises the further question of whose leisure was a problem to whom. This chapter addresses this question, and describes the ways in which freely accessible public libraries were seen to be one means of resolving this problem.

The Industrial Revolution and popular leisure

Popular leisure activity frequently presented social problems well before the nineteenth century, for, as Hole,[1] and Golby and Purdue[2] show, it was a recurring feature of British history since at least the Middle Ages. Attempts to regulate or manipulate leisure were often religiously motivated, although economic factors were also important, as indeed were safety and public order in the case of rougher and more exuberant pursuits and pastimes.[3] The earliest nineteenth-century critiques of leisure were based upon religion, typified in Hannah More's attack upon the indulgent pastimes of the aristocracy which reflected the Puritan belief that recreation ought to be guided by morality.[4] However, it was only as the century progressed that popular leisure came to be considered as a serious problem, with economic and social implications.

Historians of leisure point to the Industrial Revolution as the most important factor in changing patterns of recreation in the nineteenth century. As this took place over a number of decades, changes in leisure were neither sudden nor dramatic, but evolutionary and gradual. Dumazedier's[5] description of leisure as a product of industrialization is well illustrated in the changes which occurred in leisure during this period, as the two major factors which influenced leisure development were themselves direct outcomes of industrialization, namely the factory system of production and urbanization.

Before the Industrial Revolution, England had an agrarian economy and the bulk of the working population depended for their living, directly or indirectly, upon agricultural production and the land. Popular recreation was closely integrated with the farming year as recreational opportunities, such as fairs, harvest homes, hiring fairs and Plough Mondays, were all based upon agricultural practice and served economic and social as well as individual purposes. The seasons too brought a regular cycle of parish wakes, feast days, holy days and holiday times such as Easter and Christmas which changed little from year to year. A great deal of popular leisure activity was boisterous, tended towards drunkenness and was subject to little regulation; football, for example, was not the codified game of today but a disorganized and often violent affair which usually involved scores of players and took place across acres of land. Sometimes, there were local attempts to curtail the rougher and more violent aspects of such recreation, but, as leisure did not present any serious political, social or economic threat, it tended to be tolerated within fairly liberal limits, largely because it provided a safety valve for the release of tensions. A further characteristic feature of leisure in pre-industrial society was the abuse of animals for various forms of activities now illegal; bull-running, bear-baiting, cock-fighting and dog-fighting were all widely pursued pastimes. Although popular leisure was criticized from within Puritanism and other denominational interests, and although it was occasionally necessary to curb certain excesses in the interests of the peace and of social order, it nevertheless had important benefits in stabilizing communities and in providing opportunities for the ruling classes to consolidate and maintain their dominance through patronage and tolerance.

The cataclysmic social and economic changes brought about by industrialization wrought comparable changes in leisure practice and its social significance. The most influential factors of change were the introduction of the factory system and time discipline, the altered relationship between employer and employee and the rapid urbanization which occurred in the first half of the nineteenth century. The new industrial towns were built with scant regard to the social needs of their inhabitants, and there are numerous graphic descriptions of the squalor and poverty of the living conditions endured by the working populations of these towns. Leisure opportunities were extremely limited and, due to the lack of other facilities and opportunities, the public house became a principal leisure attraction, its appeal enhanced by the damp and overcrowded conditions of domestic life. In addition to selling beer and spirits, public houses had a range of associated leisure activities which embraced animal sports, gambling, prostitution and fighting; they also served as political meeting places where radical newspapers were read, and thus gave popular leisure an association with working-class politics. The rough and sometimes violent nature of popular leisure was not in itself a new phenomenon, but, in the context of a crowded urban environment with a rapidly changing social structure, popular leisure became associated with disorder, drunkenness, violence and immorality.

There were also economic implications, for while time for leisure in agricultural England had been regulated by the seasons and by agricultural cycles, the factory system imposed a restrictive time discipline, and absenteeism or an inability to work effectively through the effects of drink were economically costly. Time discipline became of importance, not only in the sense that the working week was rigidly organized on a time basis, but also in that it became important for leisure time to be used in a way which did not disrupt or impede economic progress.[6] As the nineteenth century progressed, the drunken and immoral nature of popular leisure became of a growing social concern to the government and to industrial employers as well as to temperance reformers and evangelicals. This concern focused not upon leisure in a general sense but upon urban working-class leisure, and the major initiatives for the reform of popular leisure were subsequently aimed specifically at this sector of the population.

Throughout the 1830s and 1840s there was a steady output of journalism about the condition of the working classes in England, much of which investigated popular leisure. The Reverend P. Gaskell, writing in 1836, observed that although agricultural life in rural England was far from idyllic, it had at least provided a range of leisure opportunities other than the beer shop, whereas the factory workers of the industrial towns were obliged to rely almost exclusively on pubs, gin shops, clubs and political unions – a further instance of the association of leisure with political activity.[7] Nearly all writers who wished to learn something about the effects of industrialization visited Manchester, a city which epitomized the best and the worst results of industrialization. Though most were appalled by what they found, many were reluctant to condemn the activities they discovered outright because they realized that much of the immorality and inherent destructiveness of leisure was linked to other social factors. Kay, for instance, described how factory workers were reduced to little more than adjuncts to the machines they operated, and how ill-ventilated and damp houses were so incapable of providing an opportunity for leisure that working men were glad to escape them for the public house.[8] Engels' account of Saturday night in Manchester in the 1840s, a city in which there were an estimated 1,000 public houses, is still impressive:

> On Saturday evenings, especially when wages are paid and work stops somewhat earlier than usual, when the whole working-class pours from its own poor quarters into the main thoroughfares, intemperance may be seen in all its brutality. I have rarely come out of Manchester on such an evening without meeting numbers of people staggering and seeing others lying in the gutter. On Sunday evening the same scene is usually repeated, only less noisily.[9]

Engels did not excuse the prevailing 'intemperance and sexual licence', but he understood why working-class people sought immediate sensual gratification and an escape from reality. Another visitor to Manchester in the 1840s offered a succinct analysis of the root of the leisure problem:

> If the people of Manchester wish to go out upon a fine Sunday, where must they go? There are no public promenades, no avenues, no public gardens; and even no public common. If the inhabitants seek to breathe the pure atmosphere of the country, they are reduced to the necessity of swallowing

dust upon the public highways. Everything in the suburbs is closed against them; everything is private property. In the midst of the beautiful scenery of England, the operatives are like the Israelites of old, with the promised land before them, but forbidden to enter it. Aristocracy appropriates to itself the soil, and lives in ease and luxury, yet fears to grant a paltry plot for public recreation to the labourers, who have been the ladder to which they are indebted for their own elevation. Even the cemeteries and the Botanic Gardens are closed upon Sunday. What then remains but the brutal diversion of drunkenness?[10]

There was little disagreement that popular recreation needed to be reformed, only on how this was to be effected. There were two means of achieving this: coercively through repressive legislation to suppress socially damaging recreational activities, or, secondly and more constructively, persuasively through the provision of new and better leisure facilities and opportunities. The second of these approaches was the more significant to the introduction of public libraries.

LEISURE REFORM AND THE INTRODUCTION OF PUBLIC LIBRARIES

The campaign to reform leisure, which was in essence a series of initiatives rather than a coordinated mass movement, spanned the whole of the Victorian era. One of the earliest references to a constructive approach to recreational reform was Robert Slaney's *Essay on the beneficial direction of rural expenditure*, published in 1824.[11] Though writing in terms of rural rather than urban areas, Slaney's observation that the provision of recreational facilities for the labouring classes would be beneficial to society as a whole was adopted as a basic rationale by leisure reformers in urban areas. From the 1830s onwards, the growing interest in the reform of popular leisure was reflected in the parliamentary papers of the period. The *Report from the Select Committee on Public Walks*,[12] published in 1833, highlighted the emerging problem of working-class leisure, when it alluded to the 'low and debasing pleasures' of the working classes such as drunkenness and blood sports, and in the following year the *Report from the Select Committee on Drunkenness*[13] presented a further alarming portrayal of the nature of urban working-class recreation. Both reports pointed out that a major cause of the problem was the shortage of recreational facilities other than licensed premises. Pressure for leisure reform came from many quarters, particularly the temperance movement, which organized games, walks, excursions and other activities documented by its historian Brian Harrison.[14] Many temperance reformers placed an emphasis upon the benefits of reading, and promoted the development of temperance hotels, coffee houses and reading rooms,[15] and later the establishment of publishing houses to produce popular novels with a well-defined anti-drink moral.

Some reformers were motivated purely by moral concerns, while others had a vested interest in nurturing class harmony through a paternalistic approach to leisure provision. Lord John Manners, for example, an enthusiastic supporter of public libraries and of improved recreational facilities in general, felt that it was important to 'show the people, i.e. the lower orders, by adding to their comforts and pleasures, in the only legitimate way a legislative can do, viz. by voting money to build public baths, to keep up, or rather to restore public games, to form public walks, that we are their real friends'.[16]

The benefits of improving popular leisure through the provision of appropriate facilities were thus widely recognized by various groups, and the concept of 'rational recreation' emerged. Again, although not an organized movement in the sense of a political or moral campaign, rational recreation was, in the words of a modern leisure historian, an attempt to forge more effective behavioural constraints through leisure.[17] It embodied an idealism which sought to promote morality and sobriety in popular leisure, and to bring working-class leisure activities into line, and where possible into contact, with middle-class leisure. It was tremendously influential not only in the introduction of public libraries, but in the ways in which libraries, when they were established, approached the provision of recreational reading.

Libraries as agents for leisure reform

There are many instances of publicly available libraries being suggested as a means of reforming working-class leisure before their introduction in 1850, one of the earliest being that by Robert Slaney, who devoted a chapter to libraries in his above-mentioned book.[18] Slaney identified two principles which became widely accepted: namely, that public libraries were to be provided principally for the benefit of working people, and that they would offer a viable recreational alternative by providing the working classes with 'some easy and attractive occupation for their leisure hours, so that they might be tempted from the tavern or the theatre, to which they are now almost compelled to resort, for want of any place of rational amusement'. These libraries were to be maintained by donations from the rich, in whose 'interest' it would be to do so.

A similar persuasive approach to recreational reform is found in Herschel's address[19] at the opening of the Windsor public library and reading room (not a rate-supported library) nine years later in which he linked libraries with the problem of leisure when he said that the establishment of the library was welcome because 'There is a gentle, but perfectly irresistible coercion in a habit of reading well-directed over the whole tenor of a man's character and conduct, which is not the less effective because it works insensibly'. Herschel was aware that the habit of reading would only spread if appealing literature were easily available, and, although he felt that the library ought not to provide popular fiction, he thought that novels of the 'utmost purity and morality' with a potential to improve those who read them, such as those by Cervantes, Richardson and Scott, could usefully be stocked.

The potential benefits of public libraries in recreational reform were also recognized in parliamentary circles, notably by the 1834 Select Committee on Drunkenness, which recommended that one method of reducing drunkenness would be to establish recreational facilities such as parks and gardens, and also 'district and parish libraries, museums and reading rooms, accessible at the lowest rate of charge; so as to admit of one or the other being visited in any weather, and at any time'.[20]

A more direct, albeit unsuccessful, attempt to establish public libraries as a means of recreational reform was undertaken in the following year by James Silk Buckingham, who had been Chairman of the Select Committee on Drunkenness. His *Public Institutions Bill*[21] sought to 'facilitate the formation and establishment of Public Institutions which would incorporate libraries, museums and reading rooms' and echoed the recommendation of the Select Committee on Drunkenness that such recreational facilities should be available especially in the winter months when outdoor recreation was impracticable. The function of such libraries in improving working-class leisure activity was clarified in the parliamentary debate of the Bill, when Silk Buckingham argued that they would be places of recreation 'free from the temptation of strong drink', and would thus 'have a tendency to raise the moral habits of the working classes'.[22]

The 1849 Select Committee on Public Libraries and the Public Libraries Act 1850

By the late 1840s interest in public libraries had grown sufficiently to establish a Parliamentary Select Committee to investigate their feasibility. There appeared to be no single argument for public libraries which was strong enough in itself, and thus their case was constructed upon various perceived outcomes, among them education, technical and economic advancement and parity with a number of European countries with allegedly better public access to libraries than Great Britain. However, a major recurring theme in the evidence of witnesses was the role that libraries could play in maintaining social order and promoting moral values by providing better recreational opportunities for urban working-class populations. A brief reference to a small selection of this evidence illustrates this.

Edward Edwards was convinced that libraries would do this, and believed they should be established because ' . . . even apart from the direct instruction which may in that way be brought within the reach of the people, the means of rational amusement, which would by that means be open to them, would be exceedingly important'.[23] The need for rational amusement was needed, according to Edwards, because 'the want of some provision, from the public resources, of amusements of a rational and improving character, has led to the introduction, to a large extent in our towns, of brutalizing and demoralizing amusements. In my opinion, something ought to have been done long before to obviate that evil, and the necessity that something of the kind should now be done is very urgent'.[24]

George Dawson, a non-conformist minister and lecturer who was later to play a key role in the adoption of the Public Libraries Acts in Birmingham, also spoke of the role of public libraries in encouraging reading as a recreational alternative to drunkenness, bull-baiting and dog-fighting,[25] and Samuel Smiles thought they would be useful rational recreational facilities which would encourage working men to stay at home to read.

In the parliamentary debate of William Ewart's Public Libraries Bill, the likelihood that public libraries would be used for recreational rather than educational purposes provided the opposition with a convenient line of attack which has been deployed by critics of libraries ever since. It was also said that public libraries would not appeal to working-class readers and that they would quickly degenerate into newsrooms patronized by those sufficiently wealthy to have ample leisure time.[26] However, the allegations that libraries would be used largely for leisure purposes were turned around by the Bill's supporters, who emphasized the benefits of providing a socially supportive form of recreational facility for working-class men and women. Robert Slaney, who had suggested the formation of public libraries more than a quarter of a century earlier, argued that libraries would cost far less than the idleness and crime which was so prevalent because of the lack of recreational facilities,[27] while Joseph Brotherton also supported the Bill because libraries would be 'the cheapest police that could possibly be established'.[28]

Public libraries were thus established without a clear mandate, for, while their educational benefits were undoubtedly of importance in securing their introduction, it was simultaneously recognized that they had a potentially vital role in leisure reform. The imprecise and sometimes conflicting concepts of public library purpose were exacerbated by the fact that there was a widespread belief that public libraries would be similar to the libraries of Mechanics' Institutes, with the difference that they would be free. However, because, even by this relatively early date, Mechanics' Institutes had deviated from their original aims, this served not to clarify the confusion but to deepen it.

Mechanics' Institutes, fiction and recreation

Although they were established primarily with educational objectives, Mechanics' Institutes gradually became more orientated to recreation than to education, and this influenced the growth of public libraries in a number of ways. First, Mechanics' Institute libraries not only provided a model upon which public libraries could style themselves, but many public libraries took over the bookstocks of Mechanics' Institute libraries, inheriting novels and other works of imaginative literature in the process. Several public libraries thus acquired an instant bookstock with an inherent recreational appeal. Second, the popularity of the Mechanics' Institute libraries encouraged the habit of using libraries for obtaining recreational reading, and it seems likely that some custom would have been transferred from the Mechanics' Institute to the public library when a takeover occurred. Third, although both Mechanics' Institute and public libraries were expected by their governing bodies and by their librarians to place an emphasis upon technical and educational books, the pressure of public demand gradually forced them into providing a recreation-orientated service.

At the time of the Public Libraries Act of 1850 there were some 700 Mechanics' Institutes, with an approximate total membership of 120,000.[29] It was originally intended that Mechanics' Institutes would be for the benefit of the working class, but, as early as 1836, Gaskell found that 'Few, indeed, of their numbers are from the class they are chiefly designed to benefit',[30] and a few years later Samuel Smiles claimed that Mechanics' Institutes had become, for the most part, institutes of the 'middle and respectable classes'.[31] Along with middle-class patronage came a change from educational priorities to a recreational service which was reflected in Institute libraries, which, by 1877, were said to be 'almost entirely devoted to the supply of fiction and popular books of travel, while books of reference, works in art, science and general literature scarcely find a place on their shelves'.[32] This assertion is clearly supported by some Mechanics' Institute library issue statistics; fiction accounted for 64.6% of the issue at Manchester and 77.5% at Leeds,[33] and reports from other towns show a comparable trend. This gradual drift to recreational provision did not pass unnoticed, and many of the concerns which were voiced in respect of the Mechanics' Institutes were later repeated by critics of the provision of fiction in public libraries. These included fears about the morality of popular novels, the suspicion that sensation novels would undermine intentions to borrow educational books, and a feeling that fiction detracted from the serious educational image of Mechanics' Institutes.[34]

On the other hand, the provision of fiction and recreational literature in Mechanics' Institute libraries was not always viewed disparagingly. In his *Manual for Mechanics' Institutes*, published in 1839, Francis Baldwin Duppa,[35] acknowledged that some amusement was essential to the working classes if each man were to become a 'useful, active or contented member of society', and recommended that recreational provision should be a priority in Mechanics' Institutes. Hole, too, thought that recreation was important and supported the inclusion of 'moderate and rational amusement'.[36] Thus, by the time of the Public Libraries Act of 1850, Mechanics' Institutes had a significant recreational role which continued to expand so much that, by the end of the century, Thomas Greenwood concluded that amusement and recreation had usurped their educational role to the point at which many had degenerated into 'little more than respectable lounges'.[37]

THE LEISURE USES OF EARLY PUBLIC LIBRARIES

The lack of a clear set of objectives, together with the absence of a model upon which to base themselves, meant that public libraries attempted to be all things to all men. There were no national standards or guidelines to assist in the formulation of priorities at a local level, and library development was piecemeal and largely reactive. Education was certainly an important element of the library service, and from the start reference libraries were established, thus indicating that councils and library committees had firm ideas about the library's educational functions. However, the public demand for fiction and other recreational material was an equally established feature, and both lending and reference departments had a significant amount of leisure use.

Although it is difficult to quantify precisely the leisure use of public libraries, because then, as now, issues showed only a partial picture, there is no doubt that leisure was of major importance. Fiction and other recreational literature were provided for reading both at home or on the premises from the beginning. It is worth noting that this was anticipated, for Edward Edwards, commenting upon Manchester's public library, acknowledged that it had been foreseen before the library opened that a 'good provision of Prose Fiction' would be needed.[38] It was common practice to provide novels in both lending and reference departments. At Manchester, the aggregate issue of the reference department between 1852 and 1857 included over 160,000 books from the Literature and Polygraphy class, approximately one-third of these issues being novels; in the Manchester lending department in the same period, three-quarters of the issues were from this same class, four-fifths being novels.[39] Liverpool, in particular, was well-known for its high issues of fiction; in 1868, its reference department alone issued 189,841 novels and romances, a fact which prompted Edwards to comment that, for every novel-reader in Manchester, Liverpool could boast ten.[40] A similar emphasis on fiction and recreational literature is evident in other early public libraries; Sheffield's lending department issue for 1856–7, for example, included 51.5% miscellaneous and fiction titles, rising to 56.6% in 1858–9. In Birmingham, the central library's total issue for 1868 included 73.5% of books from the Literature and Polygraphy class, which incorporated novels; in the branch libraries, this proportion was considerably higher at 85.9% at Adderly Park and 79.1% at Deritend.[41]

The categorization of library holdings in the pre-Dewey era tended to obscure the exact proportions of fiction in statistics of bookstocks and of issues. Nevertheless, a reasonably accurate measure of these can be obtained from various sources. The Parliamentary Returns of Public Libraries for 1876–7 show clearly that there was an extensive demand for novels.[42] A few examples of the domination of issues by fiction may be cited from this source: Birmingham lending department 57.16% fiction; Exeter lending department 80%; Heywood library 64.4%; Leeds 72.49%. Other sources show a similar pattern elsewhere: at Coventry, fiction never accounted for less than 63% of the total issue between 1869 and 1879, and in fact reached a peak of 80% in 1875 following a substantial stock input of novels,[43] while at Preston, the fiction issue remained at a constant 65.7% to 66.5% between 1884 and 1892.[44] A more extensive picture of fiction provision is given in a comparative table of public libraries in 22 towns, published in the *Fortnightly review* in 1889, in which prose fiction accounted for less than 50% of the total issue in only three libraries, whereas it accounted for 60% and over in 18 libraries, and for over 75% in nine of these.[45] The demand for fiction was thus substantial and, in places where the fiction issue was low, this was nearly always because of a shortage of supply rather than a lack of demand.[46]

The reactions of both the library profession and the general public to the demand for and the provision of fiction in public libraries were varied, and formed the basis of the Great Fiction Question, one of the most bitterly contested debates in public library history.

Games and smoking rooms

It is worth noting in passing that public libraries had other important recreational aspects which extended their leisure dimension.[47] Many libraries provided newsrooms in which newspapers and magazines were available, but, because such rooms attracted tramps and 'loafers', they were, in general, disliked by librarians. A further source of embarrassment to librarians was that newsrooms were frequently centres of betting activity, and were therefore deeply suspected for their associations with gambling, off-course betting being illegal. This gave rise to the notorious practice of blacking out the racing news in papers, and to a good deal of righteous indignation from the public, all of which tended to cast the librarian in the role of moral guardian and public censor. A further and generally less well-known aspect of recreational provision in public libraries before the First World War is that of games, smoking and conversation rooms. Although a number of these rooms were purpose-built, it was more commonly the case that they were inherited when public libraries were established in existing institutions such as Mechanics' Institutes. Very few games rooms survived beyond the turn of the century, mainly because they were seen to be irrelevant if not indeed injurious to the workings and image of public libraries; as Thomas Greenwood observed, a billiard room would always be a stronger inducement for use than a reference library or a newsroom.[48] There was also the associated problem of gambling, which provided libraries with a further reason for discontinuing the provision of such rooms.

Smoking rooms were introduced in a small number of libraries as a way of attracting people who might not otherwise have visited them. Chorley library's smoking room, which was opened in 1899, was built with impeccable rational recreational credentials as an alternative attraction to public houses; here, men were welcome to sit to read newspapers (newsrooms often provided standing accommodation only), and to smoke. This experiment soon proved to be a failure, however, the librarian complaining that the room attracted the rougher elements whose conversation could be heard in the rest of the library.[49] Although smoking and games rooms were not as common a feature as newsrooms, and therefore less frequently discussed in the professional press, they were nevertheless important aspects of public library leisure provision, and might have developed along different lines had it been possible to accommodate their leisure function within the evolving professional ideology of public librarianship.

Attitudes to the provision of recreational facilities in public libraries

Attitudes to the recreational uses of public libraries were varied. Initially, there was much opposition to public libraries from the agricultural and brewing lobbies, as farmers and publicans were likely to suffer if libraries were to succeed in providing a more popular leisure attraction than the public house; conversely, temperance reformers welcomed libraries for similar reasons. By the later decades of the nineteenth century, there was a wider social acceptance, not always shared by the library profession, that public libraries had a valid role in the provision of recreational opportunities, a point of view often based upon the established concept of libraries as an antidote to drunkenness and crime. In 1876, the *Saturday review* argued that public libraries ought to provide recreational reading,[50] and only a few years later James Odell wrote that recreational provision was in fact the most important aspect of their work: '... the first important work of a Free Library [is] that of employing the leisure time of the working-classes in a more rational way, and weaning them from the degrading haunts of drink and Vice ... '.[51]

Other critics saw public libraries as an aid to social stability. Lady John Manners supported libraries with the following anecdote:

> Nottingham is rich in libraries. Among many gratifying facts connected with them, I heard that, a short time after one had been established in a very low part of the town, a policeman said to a lady 'Why, ma'am, you could hardly know the place again since that room was set up' ... many believe that if the State spent more money on reading and newsrooms and libraries, far less would be expended on police stations, prisons and poor houses.[52]

Jevons, too, saw the provision of recreation through libraries as a tool for social reform,[53] and even Thomas Greenwood conceded that recreational reading might contest the attraction of the public house, noting that otherwise there would be 'infinitely more to pay in repressive organisations'.[54]

It was the provision of fiction, however, which formed the basis not only of the bulk of leisure use of public libraries, but, in quantitative terms, the greatest overall use. The debate which emerged through the practice of stocking popular novels in public libraries was complex in nature, being on one level a fairly simple argument about whether libraries should be concerned with recreation, but at a deeper level a question of the function of popular leisure and of cultural values in fiction. Before exploring the treatment of popular fiction in public libraries, the next chapter considers the social context of popular recreational reading during the period under discussion.

NOTES AND REFERENCES TO CHAPTER 2

1   Hole, C., *English sports and pastimes*, Batsford, 1949.
2   Golby, J. M. and Purdue, A. W., *The civilization of the crowd: popular culture in England 1750–1900*, Batsford, 1984, Chapter 2.
3   See Malcolmson, R., *Popular recreations in English society 1700–1850*, Cambridge University Press, 1973.
4   More, Hannah, *An estimate of the religion of the fashionable world*, London,

1818; see also: *Thoughts on the importance of the manners of the great*, London, 1818.

5   Dumazedier, J., *Towards a society of leisure*, Collier Macmillan, 1967.

6   See Thompson, E. P., 'Time, work-discipline and industrial capitalism', *Past and present*, **38**, December 1967, 56–97.

7   Gaskell, P., *Artisans and machinery: the moral and physical condition of the manufacturing population considered with reference to mechanical substitutes for human labour*, 1836, reprinted by Frank Cass, 1968, 13–112.

8   Kay, J. P., *The moral and physical condition of the working classes employed in the cotton manufacture in Manchester*, reprinted by E.J. Morten, Manchester, 1969.

9   Engels, Frederick, *The condition of the working-class in England in 1844*, Allen & Unwin, 1892, 124–33.

10 Faucher, M. L, *Manchester in 1844; its present condition and future prospects*, Simpkin, Marshall, 1844, 54–6.

11 Slaney, R., *Essay on the beneficial direction of rural expenditure*, Longman, 1824.

12 Great Britain, *Report from the Select Committee on Public Walks*, 1833.

13 Great Britain, *Report from the Select Committee on Inquiry into Drunkenness*, 1834.

14 Harrison, B., *Drink and the Victorians: the temperance question in England 1815–1872*, Faber, 1971, Chapter 14.

15 See, for example, *The Star of Temperance*, **1**, 1836; Duncan, *The temperance orator; comprising speeches, readings, dialogues and illustrations of the evils of intemperance . . . in prose and verse*, Wakefield, W. Nicholson, 18–.

16 Whibley, C., *Lord John Manners and his friends. Volume One*, Blackwood, 1925.

17 Bailey, P., *Leisure and class in Victorian England: rational recreation and the contest for control 1830–1885*, Routledge and Kegan Paul, 1978, 170. See also: Delves, A., 'Popular recreation and social conflict in Derby, 1800–1850', in Yeo, E. and Yeo, S., (eds.), *Popular culture and class conflict 1500–1914: explorations in the history of labour and leisure*, Harvester Press, 1981, 88–127.

18 Slaney, op. cit., ref. 11.

19 Herschel, J., 'An address to the subscribers to the Windsor and Eton public library and reading room, 29 January 1833', in Herschel, J., *Essays from the Edinburgh and Quarterly reviews*, Longman, 1857.

20 Great Britain, *Report from the Select Committee on Inquiry into Drunkenness*, 1834.

21 Public Institutions Bill 1835, reprinted in Kelly, T., *A history of public*

libraries in Great Britain 1845–1975, Library Association, 1975, Appendix 2, 458–64.

22 Great Britain, House of Commons, *Parliamentary debates* (Hansard), 3rd series, **30**, 1835, 651–3.

23 Great Britain, *Report from the Select Committee on Public Libraries*, 1849, q.452.

24 Great Britain, op. cit., ref. 23, q.452.

25 Great Britain, op. cit., ref. 23, q.1273–6.

26 Great Britain, House of Commons, *Parliamentary debates* (Hansard), 3rd series, **CIX**, 1850, cols. 838–51.

27 ibid.

28 ibid.

29 Tylecote, M., *The Mechanics' Institutes of Lancashire and Yorkshire before 1851*, Manchester University Press, 1957.

30 Gaskell, op. cit., ref. 7, 249.

31 *Report from Select Committee on Public Libraries*, q.1956.

32 Wright, W., On the best means of promoting the free library movement in small towns and villages, *Proceedings of the Conference of Librarians, London 1877*, 22–8. For further details of fiction provision in Mechanics' Institute libraries, see: Hole, J., *An essay on the history and management of literary, scientific and mechanics' institutions*, Longman, 1853, reprinted by Frank Cass, 1970.

33 Hanson, J., 'Free public libraries', *Westminster review*, **98**, 1872, 333–77.

34 Tylecote, op. cit., ref. 29.

35 Duppa, F. B., *A manual for Mechanics' Institutes*, Society for the Diffusion of Useful Knowledge, 1839.

36 Hole, op.cit., ref. 32.

37 Greenwood, T., *Public libraries*, Cassell, 4th edn, 1894.

38 Edwards, E., *Free town libraries*, Trubner, 1869, 78.

39 Edwards, op. cit., ref. 38, Chapter 4.

40 Edwards, op. cit., ref. 38, 122

41 Edwards, op. cit., ref. 38, 127–56.

42 Great Britain, *Parliamentary returns of public libraries 1876–7*.

43 Odell, W., 'Free libraries and their working', *Macmillans magazine*, April 1881, 439–51.

44 Preston Free Public Library, *Annual reports 1884–1892*.

45 Gattie, W. M., 'What English people read', *Fortnightly review*, **46**, 1889, 302–21.

46 Ingram, J., 'A day's reading at the Mitchell Library, Glasgow', *Library*, **1**, 1889, 281–92.

47 See: Snape, R., 'Betting, billiards and smoking: leisure in public

libraries', *Leisure studies*, **11**, 1992, 187–99.

48 Greenwood, T., *Public libraries*, op. cit., ref. 37 Chapter 27.

49 *Library Association record*, 1901, 125–7.

50 'Free libraries', *Saturday review*, **42**, 7 October 1876, 441–2.

51 Odell, W., 'Free libraries and their working', *Macmillans magazine*, April 1881, 439–51.

52 Manners, Lady J., *Encouraging experiences of free libraries, reading and recreation rooms*, Blackwood, 1886.

53 Jevons, W. Stanley, 'The rationale of free public libraries', *Contemporary review*, **39**, 1891, 385–402.

54 Greenwood, op. cit., ref. 37.

Chapter 3

Popular Recreational Reading in the Nineteenth Century

THE SOCIAL AND CULTURAL CONTEXT OF THE FICTION QUESTION

To explain the treatment of fiction in public libraries solely with reference to the attitudes and approaches of the library profession would not yield an accurate account of what happened, nor, more importantly, of why it happened. A more revealing analysis of the ways in which public libraries handled popular fiction emerges if library practice is evaluated in the context of the literary culture of the period, which was itself closely integrated with political and economic structures. No other aspect of the public library service before 1914 reveals the relationships between libraries and their social context as clearly as the treatment of fiction, because the concern about what people read in their leisure time was a widely discussed social question. As Richard Garnett wrote: '. . . there never before was so much interest and curiosity respecting the makers of books, authors, and the emitters of books, publishers, or the custodians of books, librarians'.[1] He could equally have added to this list the readers of books, for the question of who read what and with what effect was at the centre of this discussion.

Unlike most aspects of public library activity, the fiction question engaged the interest of the general public, not only because it was part of a more general social debate about recreational reading and, in a wider sense, about popular leisure activity, but because it had the added spice that when public libraries took a high moral stance on which novels to provide or not to provide, they were in effect making themselves public watchdogs or censors, and then as now this inevitably aroused interest and resentment. The fiction question was naturally discussed intensively in the professional library press, but national, and even local, newspapers frequently covered the subject in considerable depth. By 1909, the 'great fiction question' had become for at least one writer the 'great fiction bore',[2] but it was nevertheless vigorously pursued until the outbreak of the First World War, remaining even then unresolved.

What exactly was meant by 'fiction'? Categorizations such as 'literature and polygraphy' or 'light literature' which were initially used by public libraries, were unhelpful in identifying exactly which books were implied by 'fiction'. Peter Cowell, librarian of the Liverpool Free Library, attempted to clarify this by defining fiction as 'novels and romances – as distinct from poetry, drama, fables parables, fairy tales and the like',[3] but this definition does not adequately explain the complex nature of the fiction debate nor why it should have been so fiercely contested. A more analytical definition was supplied by Thomas Greenwood,who interpreted fiction as a generic term comprising not only 'questionable productions', but also 'the work of writers, the circulation of whose novels might still wisely be promoted at the cost of the town's common purse, for they are among the most skilful and persuasive of moral and intellectual educators, and they supply the moral recreation of the highest value to any community'.[4]

The fiction question was thus not simply about whether novels should be provided in public libraries, but was concerned with the distinctions between different types of novels, and with literary merit and moral standards. This in itself had further implications, for, by the later decades of the nineteenth century, the novel had become a major cultural form, and was, as Malcolm Bradbury says, a central means of exploring the state of the nation and of conveying cultural values.[5] The fiction question did not arise suddenly, but was the result of a durable concern about popular reading which had existed since at least the 1830s as a part of the 'problem' of leisure.

Reading and the problem of popular leisure

Much, though not all, of the nineteenth-century concern about popular reading was specifically about working-class reading. This concern gathered momentum in the 1830s and 1840s as the spread of literacy made the publication of popular newspapers and cheap periodical literature an increasingly attractive commercial proposition. The mid-nineteenth century reading public could be divided and categorized in a number of ways, but perhaps the most meaningful distinction was that between the respectable and the non-respectable, which translated roughly to a broad distinction between the middle- and the working-class reading publics. This is a much simplified division, and many readers of working-class origin crossed the divide to respectable literature and sought self-improvement and educational advancement, but nevertheless, in the vast majority of cases, it was a distinction which held true.

A good proportion of the popular fiction of the early nineteenth century was not written primarily with the objective of attaining mass sales to a working-class readership, and novels written towards the close of the eighteenth century, such as Mrs Radcliffe's *The mysteries of Udolpho*, and fashionable tales written in the 1830s, such as Pierce Egan's *Life in London; or, the sprees of Tom and Jerry*, were widely read yet did not cause undue concern. However, as literacy spread so did the market for 'penny' fiction and cheap novels, and the demand for fiction became endemic among working-class readers. To meet this demand, there were numerous small and cheap circulating libraries which specialized in providing such publications to working class readers. A survey of some such libraries in working-class areas of London in the 1830s revealed that moral and religious novels comprised 2.27% of their stocks, and those by Captain Marryat, Cooper and Washington Irving 5.24%; in contrast, 20% were of well-known fashionable novels and 46% were 'novels of the lowest character, being chiefly imitations of fashionable novels, containing no good, although probably nothing decidedly bad'.[6]

Writers and publishers sought to make substantial profits by producing cheap, undemanding and escapist literature to provide for this market. Some of this cheap literature was respectable, but there were many books and periodicals with a sharper edge, sometimes with republican overtones, which had a low regard for royalty, the establishment, and conventional moral standards.[7] One of the more notorious examples of this type of fiction, Reynolds' *The mysteries of London*, frequently satirized the monarchy and aristocracy; the following description of a night at the opera is a typical example: 'In the Royal Box Queen Victoria and the Duchess of Kent were seated: behind them stood several lords and ladies in waiting – those obsequious hangers-on of Royalty who are more contemptible in their grovelling sycophancy than the most servile toad-eaters and lick-spittles are in a less elevated sphere of life'.[8]

Much of the hostile reaction to the *Mysteries* was based upon the fear that this, and publications like it, would undermine respect for authority in the young readers it would inevitably attract, and would delude them by its 'false social and political economy'.[9] A further notorious example of popular cheap fiction, *Varney the vampire*, which was published in weekly penny editions, was taken to task by a contemporary critic for pandering to the lowest taste purely for commercial gain by being a work of an 'unhealthy moral tendency', produced in harmony with the worst instincts of human nature.[10] Publications of this nature were enormously popular among working-class readers, though they remained largely unknown to the respectable middle-class reading public, and contributed to the growth of a sub-species of literary production which was far removed from the literary world of quarterly reviews, three-decker novels and circulating libraries such as Mudie's. As one observer noted, the reading of artisans and manual workers was of a class which hardly ever came under the notice of the 'person of average culture'.[11]

The social concerns about the recreational reading of the working classes were a major theme of the report of the 1849 Select Committee on Public Libraries. One witness spoke of the many inferior novels popular amongst the working class, including translations of French novels, with a tendency to 'pervert the mind'.[12] John Imray, a witness called before the committee, described them as '. . . periodicals containing horrible stories, with much of the marvellous and a good deal of the disgusting in them; one sort of book which seems to be sought very much by that class are memoirs of notorious rogues, and extracts from the *Newgate calendar*, all of which have the very worst tendency; perhaps a worse tendency than books positively indecent or immoral'.[13] It was argued by the public library's supporters that libraries would do much to eradicate these patterns of reading by providing more socially beneficial forms of recreational literature.

There was strong support for public libraries from the temperance movement, within which there had been a long-standing desire to improve the moral standard of popular reading. In 1831, Joseph Livesey published the first issue of the *Moral reformer*, a journal committed to the improvement of the moral welfare of the industrial working classes of the new towns. A later series of articles in the *Band of Hope journal*[14] explored the uses of fiction in promoting both temperance and rational recreation and pointed to the dual nature of reading – immoral books were a 'poison to the soul and corruption to the heart' but good books were the basis of mental improvement and a well-balanced character. By the 1860s such rigidly held attitudes to fiction had softened, but the temperance journal *Meliora* still urged a degree of caution by reminding its readers that recreational reading had a purpose beyond simple amusement: 'Reading is only useful as it enlarges and invigorates the mental faculties . . . light, wholesome and innocent reading for the purposes of recreation is, if pursued in moderation, promotive of the health of both mind and body'.[15]

There was a minority view that fiction in itself was a bad thing. One book of Christian instruction for youth admonished its young readers in austere terms: 'Novels, plays and love poems are also a fertile source of impurity – a pest of corruption to the mind and heart. The reading of romances which treat of intrigues, or irreligious books, will inflict such deep wounds in your soul as may prove incurable'.[16] A similar attack appeared in the *Church of England's quarterly review* in 1842, which claimed that much harm and little good had been done by modern novels, especially those which portrayed crime or vice in less than most condemnatory fashion.[17] As time progressed, religious denunciations of novels became less frequent, a major change in attitude being marked by the first serialization of a novel in the *Wesleyan magazine* in 1877,[18] while Congregationalists, who had a particularly active interest in popular recreation, adopted a less restrictive approach to novels when they conceded that though some novels were indeed corrupt and injurious, others could be instructive and improving.[19]

THE MARKET FOR FICTION

From their introduction in 1850 to the early years of the twentieth century, public libraries operated in a society that was both curious and anxious about popular reading. In the later Victorian period, the demand for entertaining and amusing fiction increased following the Education Act 1870 which provided compulsory primary education for everyone and ensured that literacy, which had begun to spread, continued to do so. The expansion of the reading public provided a boost to mass popular publishing and, as a contemporary critic observed: 'Publishers are now beginning to awaken to the fact that the spread of education and the increased facilities of communication have created a vast new public to which it is worthwhile to appeal'.[20] Publishing fiction became a commercially attractive venture, reflected in the increase in the number of authors, journalists and editors in Great Britain from around 3,400 in 1881 to around 14,000 in 1911. By the end of the nineteenth century, there were over 400 publishing houses in London alone.[21] In terms of novels produced, the statistics tell an equally impressive tale: 381 new novels published in 1850, 969 in 1886 and 1,825 in 1899. This expansion in publishing revitalized interest in popular working-class reading, and contemporary reviewing publications discussed this topic regularly. This investigation of popular fiction and its readership bears some comparisons with twentieth-century moral panics about television and popular music, and was characterized by evocative terminology, typified in *British quarterly review*'s description of the 'flood' of cheap literature then becoming available: even the word 'cheap' had connotations beyond mere cost.[22]

As the market for popular fiction expanded, so did the number of authors hoping to cater for it. Many of these are now forgotten, but several were exceptionally popular in their own lifetimes. Writers such as Mary Braddon, Mrs Henry Wood, James Payn and Rhoda Broughton achieved huge sales and mass readerships, and their works formed the backbone of many public library lending departments. Although a relatively small number of novelists, Scott and Dickens for instance, had amassed a fortune through writing prior to the emergence of these writers, this had not been common. However, from the 1860s onwards, novel writing became an increasingly attractive way of earning significant sums of money. Mary Braddon, who was virtually forced into writing to support herself and her mother, was one of the first popular novelists to achieve success in this way, and her fourth and most well-known novel *Lady Audley's secret*, published in 1862, achieved immense sales. Many of these authors were exceptionally prolific; Braddon published over 67 novels between 1862 and 1913, while Mrs Henry Wood, who published a similar number, attained total sales of over two and a half million by 1898, with one novel alone, *East Lynne*, going to 430,000 printings by that year. In her novel *A lost ideal*, Annie Swan depicted the pressures many such novelists must have experienced concerning their continuing creativity, when her heroine-novelist expresses a sentiment which was doubtlessly widely shared by contemporary literary critics, though not, apparently, by readers: 'You see . . . I've been at it so long, my ideas have got a little thin. This is my thirty-seventh three volume novel, Mr. Woodgate – think of that'.[23]

This 'new' popular fiction was eagerly devoured by readers, but was greeted cautiously, and often with hostility, by literary critics. Most of it was written with no claim to literary merit, though it was obviously appealing in terms of plot and style, and was considered by reviewers and, as we shall see later, by many librarians to be inherently inferior to respectable mainstream fiction. This negative attitude to popular fiction continued to flourish into the twentieth century and is not yet extinct today. It was based not solely on artistic and literary merit, but seems to have stemmed from the fact that this fiction was enjoyed by millions of readers and had a mass rather than an elite appeal. Literary and highbrow reviews felt it was their function to inform their educated readers of this vast sub-stratum of popular literature, the authors of which were not, as one critic expressed it, 'among those which appear in the Athenaeum and the Spectator', and whose works were not within the canon of 'high class fiction read by cultured and leisured people'.[24] The reading public, which had certainly not been homogeneous prior to this, became markedly more fragmented and the gap between the respectable middle-class reading public and the newly evolving working-class reading public widened. The cultural distinctions between literary and popular fiction were further emphasized in descriptions of the vast readership for allegedly immoral and sensational publications, which often implied that literature read by poor and ill-educated people could hardly be worthwhile. There was also a worry that reading such fiction might induce criminal activity; for example, in 1867, the *Saturday review* defined the popular novel as a 'medium through which moral poison is frequently administered' and connected increases in social and domestic crime with those in depravity in popular fiction.[25] Although no connection was proven, this view was long-lived, and even 30 years later an article on 'low' fiction in the *Westminster review*[26] claimed that fiction portraying vice exerted a criminal influence upon its readers, and commented that public libraries could do much to overcome this by elevating reading tastes.

Morality and respectable fiction

Morality and respectability were essential qualities in any novel which was to meet the approval of the literary critics. Although similar in many aspects, they were not synonymous. A respectable novel could be read by the whole family – father, mother, son and daughter – with no risk of taint or indecency. Morality in fiction was open to subjective opinion. One measure was the extent to which a novel engendered in the reader a sympathy for action considered, by contemporary standards, to be immoral. One critic clarified this by comparing Fielding, a moral writer who did not seek the reader's sympathy for his hero's 'lapses from virtue', with Defoe, who was an immoral writer for doing the opposite.[27] Fielding may have been a moral writer, but by the mid-nineteenth century he was no longer considered to be a respectable writer, and *Tom Jones* was not the type of novel the average Victorian middle class family would place on its sitting room bookshelf. In simple terms, good fiction offered moral guidance and instruction to the reader, and would not disturb sensibilities. This was an important distinction in differentiating good fiction from bad, and was considered of greater significance than its ability to entertain the reader. Archibald Sparke, the librarian at Carlisle, felt that as the first object of every novelist was to instruct and amuse, the question then arose as to which works instructed most, as the provision of amusement was 'not a matter of primary importance'. Hence, some novels were bad because they glorified immoral actions and made heroes of villains, and even established authors nowadays considered as minor classical novelists, were guilty:

> Two of the most popular authors of the nineteenth century have been mainly responsible for such literature. Ainsworth delights one with his splendid descriptions of life and manners, and Lytton will always live as one of our most finished and accomplished writers, and though I am convinced neither of them would have wilfully produced books the results of which are deplorable, there can be no question that *Jack Sheppard*, *Paul Clifford*, and *Eugene Aram* have had an influence which every right-thinking man must regret. Criminals of the worst type are converted into popular heroes. The *Newgate calendar* can show us few more base and miserable murderers than *Eugene Aram* or few more deliberate criminals than *Jack Sheppard*, and yet these personages are made into heroes![28]

The distinction between fiction which instructed the reader and had some improving effect and that produced simply to provide relaxation or amusement is well-illustrated in the controversies around two specific fiction genres, namely French novels and sensation novels.

French novels

The popularity of translations of French novels among readers of all social classes was a much discussed topic from the 1840s onwards. In Mary Braddon's *Lady Audley's secret*, the wealthy Robert Audley always has to-hand a small collection of French novels with which to amuse himself, and even William Ewart, whose Public Libraries Bill resulted in the Public Libraries Act of 1850, is said to have enjoyed reading them.[29] French novels quickly acquired a notoriety, initially through their sensationalism and language, and later through their realism and frank treatment of sexual and political themes. An article on French fiction, published in *Blackwood's magazine* in 1852[30] noted that one did not normally find 'either wisdom or morality' in 'highly wrought and licentious' French novels and concluded that it was difficult to recommend French fiction suitable for English fireside family reading. In the later decades of the nineteenth century, the naturalistic French novel also received a hostile critical reception because of its refusal to idealize life; it was, in the words of one critic, a 'menace to the sense of beauty, to the power of conscience, and to all the sweeter and finer elements of imagination'.[31] John Ruskin too spoke out against these novels: 'no good to society', he said, could ever be gained through the 'pictorial representation of its diseases'.[32] This type of novel is best typified in the works of Emile Zola, and it is a measure of the strength of the British reaction to Zola that his publisher, Vizetelly, was imprisoned for three months on an obscenity charge in 1888, following the publication of *La Terre*.

French novels presented public libraries with a dilemma, for although they had an obvious educational value to those learning French, most were thought to be immoral and unsuitable for middle-class readers. Henry Guppy, the librarian of Manchester's John Rylands Library and the editor of the *Library Association record*, thought that Maupassant, Balzac and Zola should be excluded from public libraries because they had no beneficial moral influence,[33] and indeed a number of libraries did ban Zola's novels. However, Ernest Baker, a leading authority on library fiction in the early twentieth century, devised a solution which shows how attitudes to fiction were often influenced by the socio-economic status of its readers; it was to provide original copies of French novels but not translations 'in the trust that the readers who can master the French of these authors will be of mature kind and intelligent enough to receive nothing but good from the works of so much truth and sincerity'.[34]

Sensation novels

The sensation novel evolved in the 1860s and was so called because it depicted socially deviant forms of behaviour – crime, adultery and bigamy – in ordinary domestic settings and because it relied upon implausible and often bizarre plots. A modern critic has described the sensation novel as having 'a unique mixture of contemporary domestic realism with elements of the Gothic romance, the Newgate novel of criminal "low life" and the "silver fork" novel of scandalous and sometimes criminal "high life".[35] Thousands of sensation novels were published and, although only a few are remembered today, one or two of the better known examples of the genre, such as *The woman in white* by Wilkie Collins, *Lady Audley's secret* by Mary Braddon and *East Lynne* by Mrs Henry Wood, have become minor classics. A brief description of the plots of two of the more well-known sensation novels gives some idea of the style and appeal of the genre. In *Lady Audley's secret*, the heroine, believing herself to be a widow, marries the wealthy Robert Audley. When her first husband turns out to be still alive, she finds herself living in unintentional bigamy and attempts to murder him by pushing him down a well, and, thinking herself to have killed him, she returns to what is to all outward appearances a normal life. However, her husband is not killed in his fall, but only injured, and manages to escape. After a further period, he returns once more to expose her as his would-be murderer, after which she is exiled to an asylum in Belgium. Although Lady Audley's actions are clearly presented as wrong by the standards of the day, the reader is obliged to feel sympathy for her in the unlikely situation in which she finds herself. In *East Lynne*, the main character is also a woman who becomes an adulteress, again unwittingly, and is forced to flee to Europe with her lover, away from her family and children. Here, she discovers that she has been deceived and, after becoming disfigured in a railway accident, she returns home and takes employment as a governess to her own children in her old family house, though she remains, implausibly, unrecognized until just before her death in the final chapters. Once more, the reader is urged to sympathize with the heroine, who, although she abandons her husband and children for another man, is portrayed as one sinned against rather than sinning. With plots like these, delivered in a racy and easy-to-read style, it is not difficult to understand why sensation novels were popular with the reading public, even though literary critics and librarians usually wrote of them in slighting terms. Archibald Sparke, for instance, thought sensation novels were intrinsically evil, and that there were several more instructive writers of fiction:

> . . . even amongst those writers who have of recent years enjoyed the greatest popularity, no impartial observer can say that the tendency has not been evil. Take Miss Braddon's *Aurora Floyd*, or any of Miss Broughton's novels. Can anyone say with justice that their tendency is moral? . . . Thackeray said 'Everyone ought to cultivate the acquaintance of his betters', and no one can read Black, Blackmore, Dickens, Eliot, Kingsley, Meredith, Oliphant, Scott or Thackeray without feeling that they are in the company of betters, and without feeling better and wiser.[36]

Sensation novels were occasionally referred to as 'fast' novels, although, as a series of articles by Alfred Austin demonstrated, a fine distinction separated fast novels, such as those by Ouida which glorified decadence and luxury, and sensation novels which simply depended upon improbable plots in ordinary settings.[37] However, to most librarians and critics, this distinction was purely academic, and both fast and sensation novels were thought to be over-dependent on plot, lacking literary value, immoral, and likely to encourage juvenile crime.

Like many other aspects of popular recreation, sensation novels were much discussed in contemporary newspapers and journals. A critical article published in 1864 condemned the sensation novel for its obsessions with crime, bigotry and hypocrisy and its inherent dependence on a continuing heightening of these to arouse the interest of the reader,[38] while the *Christian remembrancer* saw it as a sign of the times, eager to challenge conventional standards and willing to appeal to the reader's 'lower instincts'.[39] Other critics were more accommodating and accepted sensation novels as a reasonable form of escapist recreation which, although it might have its faults, was better than some other forms.[40] As time progressed, the popularity of the sensation novel ceased to be a matter of urgent social discussion, and its potential to bring some excitement into uneventful lives became more widely valued.

THE NOVEL AND THE STATUS OF LITERARY CULTURE

It is easy, from the perspective of the telecommunications-dominated late twentieth century, to underestimate the cultural and social importance of the English novel in the period which is roughly covered between the years 1860 and 1914. Before the advent of radio and television, the printed word was the major medium of mass communication, and fiction was the primary recreational form of this medium. By the later nineteenth century, the English novel had become a major cultural form, and was associated with dominant values, morality and the social order. The great Victorian novelists identified with their readers; as Walter Allen[41] has noted, they addressed the literate public, which they interpreted in almost wholly middle-class terms, and shared their readers' preoccupations and concerns. Novelists were in harmony with the society in which they lived; if they criticized it, as they frequently did, they did so in the way in which many of their readers questioned it and, although they expressed doubts and fears about the social issues of the day, they did so from a position within society, not one alienated from it. As a modern critic has commented, fiction formed a 'connecting point between the domestic experience of most people, and the public arena of culture as a whole'; reviews of and extracts from novels were published in literary reviews and journals which themselves had explicit political and implicit ideological aims.[42] These reviews were read principally by those occupying positions of educational and economic advantage; they served, as John Gross notes, 'the interests of the most powerful section of the community',[43] and nurtured a bond between economic and political power and the literary culture and the world of books. In the words of Queenie Leavis,[44] the maintenance of cultural standards and values became the responsibility of an elite who believed that English literature was the principal agency for the preservation of cultural values, and a close relationship between culture, literature and social structure developed.

In 1865, Matthew Arnold published the first series of his *Essays in criticism* and, in 1869, at roughly the same time that the sensation novel emerged, *Culture and anarchy*[45] appeared, which explored the meanings of culture and its functions. These were influential works, linking criticism of art and literature with the role of culture in society. Arnold's interpretation of culture as a 'study of perfection, and of harmonious perfection' is widely known, but of equal interest is his view of the function of culture in combatting anarchy and social disintegration, in which English literature had a fundamental role. This view had far-reaching implications for public libraries, because if English literature and standard novels were to maintain cultural standards and support a dominant ideology, then libraries were part of the means of effecting this. The novel was revered for its role in the transmission of culture, and the following passage written in 1872, typifies the esteem in which the English novel and its principal writers were held:

> Will not all thoughtful men allow that the reading of the works of Scott, Dickens, Thackeray, Lytton, Trollope, George Eliot, Charlotte Brontë, and others, must awaken, expand and elevate every mind that can appreciate their excellencies? The indiscriminate and excessive reading of fiction may be an evil, but we venture to think that it would be an unspeakable blessing to this country if the thousands who frequent our beershops and dramshops daily and nightly were to spend a portion of their leisure time in the perusal of the writings of the authors just mentioned.[46]

It is useful, in this respect, to consider Malcolm Bradbury's argument that literature is a social product which does not only reflect society, but is a structural element within it.[47] In this perspective, literature is part of a social process through which cultural values are reproduced and a dominant ideology, or set of beliefs and traditions, is maintained; literature which challenges these may be relegated to secondary status or suppressed. As we have seen, French and sensation novels which flouted conventional mores were widely disliked by literary professionals, and even fiction with higher artistic value, for example, novels by George Moore and Thomas Hardy, which embodied an intellectual reaction to the conventions and assumptions of the age and did not conform to what was considered to be a norm, was widely criticized and, in some cases, banned by public libraries. At Birkenhead public library, novels by Fielding and Smollett were not usually available 'unless for persons who may be known to the librarian',[48] and works by these authors were also on restricted issue in Dewsbury.[49] There are numerous instances of public libraries banning novels: H. G. Wells' *Ann Veronica* was withdrawn from circulation in Beverley in 1910, and Fielding again proved too much for a public library to handle when Doncaster banned *Tom Jones* in 1913, as it was 'not a suitable book for young people – or for old people, either, – to have access to in a free library'.[50] One Midlands library withdrew from its stock a novel by Thomas Hardy because the wife of a member of the library committee took an objection to it, while another library transferred offending novels to the reference department.[51] This sort of practice persisted for many decades, and as recently as the 1970s many libraries still had restricted issue cupboards in which novels were locked away, available to the public only upon application to the librarian.

The literary hierarchy

Critics and reviewers had the power to shape public concepts of what was good and bad in fiction, and this process was worked through the publications and journals which were read by the most powerful and economically dominant social groups. Literature and politics combined to form a potent force in literary journals, and the critic John Morley is reported to have spoken of the contributors to these publications as being entrusted with nothing less than the 'momentous task of forming national opinion'.[52] A hierarchy of novels emerged, and, to extend the analysis to the reading of novels, a hierarchy of leisure activity, in which the reading of some novels was better than the reading of others. Literary standards were determined and maintained by literary critics and publishers of reviewing periodicals, who were able to define what Ernest Baker described as a 'traditional body of precepts and judgments which, like the common law, commands the assent of the common majority of critics from generation to generation'.[53]

The concept of a literary hierarchy is frequently encountered in the discussion of fiction in the professional library press of the period, and Baker went so far as to attempt to describe a method for such a hierarchy in an article on fiction in public libraries published in 1907.[54] In this, he delineated three categories, the first of which was of authors who should be well represented in every public library, which included Balzac, Turgenev, Henry James and Conrad. The second grouping was of authors who were 'popular mediocrities and doubtful cases' who ought to be represented by a small and carefully selected range of titles, and contained some of the most popular writers of the time, such as Marie Corelli, Mary Braddon, Mrs Henry Wood and Emma Worboise. Finally, there were authors who were 'below the standard admissible' among whom he included several well-known popular novelists, such as Florence Marryat, Guy Boothby, Annie Thomas and Dick Donovan. Other librarians, too, attempted to compile groupings of novelists according to schemes of merit. Charles Wright, the librarian at Accrington, devised a system[55] which classified certain novelists as historically educational – Scott, Harrison Ainsworth, S.R. Crockett, Silas Hocking, and J.C. Smith. A second grouping of novelists offered social education – J.M. Barrie, Walter Besant, Charles Reade and Grant Allen, while in a 'lower grade' were Mary Braddon, Ouida, Mrs Henry Wood, Rhoda Broughton and Rosa Carey.

The public library's role in providing fiction thus had an importance which extended beyond the boundaries of the library profession. The fact that fiction was important and was discussed and debated in influential journals, and the contemporary interest in the popular reading of the working classes inevitably focused attention on public libraries, their borrowers, and the books they read. That public libraries drew their memberships mainly from the working and lower middle classes heightened interest in them, and it was inevitable that, under these circumstances, the provision of fiction in libraries should become such a fiercely debated topic.

NOTES AND REFERENCES TO CHAPTER 3

1   Quoted in: Ogle, J., *The free library: its history and present condition*, Allen, 1897.

2   Herdman, D.W., 'The place and treatment of fiction in public libraries', *Library assistant*, **138**, July 1909, 375-82.

3   Cowell, P., 'On the admission of fiction in free public libraries', *Transactions and proceedings of the Conference of Librarians held in London, 1877*, 60–77.

4   Greenwood, T., *Public libraries*, Cassell, 4th edn, 1894, 33.

5   Bradbury, M., *The modern British novel*, Secker and Warburg, 1993, 9.
6   Webb, R.K., 'The Victorian reading public', in *Pelican guide to English literature. Volume six: from Dickens to Hardy*, Penguin, 1958, 205–6.
7   See: Altick, R., *The English common reader: a social history of the mass reading public 1800–1900*, University of Chicago Press, 1957; Neuburg, V., *Popular literature: a history and guide*, Penguin, 1977; James, L., *Fiction for the working man 1830–1850*, Oxford University Press, 1963; Dalziel, M., *Popular fiction 100 years ago: an unexplored tract of literary history*, Cohen and Wright, 1957; Mathieson, M., *The preachers of culture: a study of English and its teachers*, Allen and Unwin, 1975.
8   Reynolds, G.W.M., *The mysteries of the Court of London*, 1, 3rd series, 37.
9   Parker, J., 'On the literature of the working classes', *Meliora, or better times to come*, 1853.
10   Parker, op.cit., ref. 9.
11   Leigh, J., 'What do the masses read?', *Economic review*, **14**, 1904, 166–77.
12   Great Britain, *Report from the Select Committee on Public Libraries, 1849*, q.2693–5.
13   op. cit., q.3215–6.
14   Wilson, G., 'The pleasures of literature', *Band of Hope journal*, **5**, 1852, 9–10; 'The choice of books', *Band of Hope journal*, op. cit., 20–1; 'Moral and intellectual culture', *Band of Hope journal*, op. cit., 33–4; 'The value of time', *Band of Hope journal*, op. cit., 52–3.
15   'Self -culture: uses of books', *Meliora*, **9** (35), 1866, 193–204.
16   *Christian instructions for youth: with edifying examples drawn from the Holy Scripture, Lives of Saints, and other authentic sources*, London, Richardson, c. 1852.
17   *Church of England's quarterly review*, **11**, 1842, 286–7.
18   Briggs, J. and Sellars, I., (eds.), *Victorian non-conformity*, Arnold, 1973.
19   *Congregationalist*, July–August 1879.
20   Hitchman, F., 'Penny fiction', *Quarterly review*, **CLXXI**, 1896, 150–71.
21   Gross, John, *The rise and fall of the man of letters*, Weidenfeld and Nicolson, 1969.
22   *British quarterly review*, 1 April 1859, 313–45.
23   Swan, Annie S., *A lost ideal*, Oliphant, Anderson and Ferrier, 1899, 293.
24   Bosanquet, H., 'Cheap literature', *Contemporary review*, **79**, 1901, 671–81.
25   'Novel reading', *Saturday review*, **23**, February 1867, 196–7.
26   Hopkins, T. M., 'A protest against low works of fiction', *Westminster review*, **149**, January 1898, 99–102.
27   Morris, M., 'Some thoughts about novels', *Macmillan's magazine*, **55**, March 1887, 359–65.

28 Sparke, A, 'The origin of the English novel 3', *Library assistant*, **2**, Oct ober 1899, 68–71.

29 Munford, W., *William Ewart M.P.*, Grafton, 1960, 122.

30 'Fictions for French firesides', *Blackwood's magazine*, **72**, November 1852, 545–53.

31 Ward, M.A., 'Recent fiction in England and France', *Macmillans magazine*, **50**, August 1884, 250–60.

32 Ruskin, J., 'Fiction fair and foul. Part 5', *Nineteenth century*, October 1881, 516–31.

33 Guppy, H., 'French fiction and French juvenile literature for the public library', *Library Association record*, 1900, 357–72.

34 Baker, E. A., 'French fiction in public libraries', *Library world*, **2**, 1899, 68–70.

35 Brantlinger, P., 'What is sensational about the sensational novel?', *Nineteenth century fiction*, **37**, 1982, 1–28.

36 Sparke, op. cit., ref. 28.

37 Austin, A., 'Our novels', *Temple bar*, **29**, July 1870, 177–94; 410–24; 488–503.

38 'The philosophy of amusement', *Meliora*, **6**, 1864, 193–210.

39 'Our female sensation novelists', *Christian remembrancer*, **46**, 1863, 209–36.

40 See: Gattie, W. M., 'What English people read', *Fortnightly review*, **46**, 1889, 302–21.

41 Allen, W., *The English novel*, Dent, 1954, Chapter 4.

42 Blake, A., 'The place of fiction in Victorian literary culture', *Literature and history*, August 1985, 203–10.

43 Gross, op. cit., ref. 21.

44 Leavis, Q.D., *Fiction and the reading public*, Chatto & Windus, 1932.

45 Arnold, M., *Culture and anarchy*, Cambridge University Press, 1960.

46 Hanson, J., 'Free public libraries', *Westminster review*, **98**, October 1872, 333–77.

47 Bradbury, M., *The social context of modern English literature*, Blackwell, 1971.

48 Johnman, W.A.P. and Kendall, M., *Report of the commission appointed to inquire into the condition and workings of free libraries in various towns in England*, 1869, Darlington.

49 Thompson, A. H., *Censorship in public libraries in the United Kingdom during the twentieth century*, Bowker, 1975.

50 ibid. (Thompson)

51 Chennell, F., 'A few words on the censor in the public library', *Library world*, **2**, 1899–1900, 316–8.

52   Houghton, W., 'Victorian periodical literature and the articulate classes', *Victorian literature*, **22** (4), Summer 1979, 289–412.
53   Baker, E.A., 'The classification of fiction (3)', *Library world*, **2**, 1899, 177–83.
54   Baker, E. A., 'The standard of fiction in public libraries', *Library Association record*, 1907, 70–80.
55   Wright, C. R., 'The selection of books for general reading', *Accrington Observer*, 27 April 1901.

Chapter 4
The Great Fiction Question

Yet she too had her pleasures, poor old auntie. She had become a great novel-reader in her old age, the public library being only ten minutes' walk from Briarbrae. During his lifetime, on some whim or other, Gran'pa Comstock had forbidden his daughters to read novels. Consequently, having only begun to read novels in 1902, Aunt Angela was always a couple of decades behind the current mode in fiction. But she plodded along in the rear, faint yet pursuing. In the nineteen-hundreds she was still reading Rhoda Broughton and Mrs. Henry Wood. In the War years she discovered Hall Caine and Mrs. Humphry Ward. In the nineteen-twenties she was reading Silas Hocking and H. Seton Merriman, and by the nineteen-thirties she had almost, but not quite, caught up with W.B. Maxwell and William J. Locke. Further she would never get. As for the post-War novelists, she had heard of them afar off, with their immorality and their blasphemies and their devastating 'cleverness.' But she would never live to read them. Walpole we know, and Hichens we read, but Hemingway, who are you?

George Orwell *Keep the aspidistra flying*

As all public libraries provided novels, the Great Fiction Question had a universal relevance. It was vehemently debated well before the establishment of the Library Association in 1877, and in later years provided the Association's meetings and conferences with an evergreen topic upon which almost every librarian held a view. On one level, the Great Fiction Question was concerned with libraries, novels and readers; at another level, it was essentially a question about the role of the public library as a provider of leisure and the concept of public sector leisure provision. The Great Fiction Question had many facets, and was closely linked to arguments about the rates, for libraries were being constantly criticized for providing fiction and other recreational reading out of the public purse. A further aspect concerned the types of novels to be provided, for, like many leisure activities, the reading of fiction had associated values, books differing in their content and moral standard, and the ways in which public libraries treated fiction were inevitably enmeshed in contemporary arguments about literary and cultural values. There were also the questions of who should select the books, and whether libraries had a right or a duty to refuse to buy certain novels. Public libraries were free to buy or not buy fiction as they wished, as they were not under the direct control of central government but managed by local councils and library committees. The members of these committees developed library services in harmony with their own values and interests, and these differed from locality to locality. Finally, although the library profession never developed a unified policy on fiction provision, it debated the topic at considerable length.and its members not infrequently found themselves at odds, in terms of book selection, with the councillors who employed them, thus raising the issue of a professional ideology in conflict with a public bureaucracy. The Great Fiction Question, which was frequently referred to as the 'fiction nuisance' by librarians, had a profound impact on the library profession, which was obliged to reassess and redefine its concepts of professional autonomy and the role of the professional librarian.

In its most basic sense, the Great Fiction Question was simply a matter of whether or not public libraries should provide novels, and although, as we shall see, there was a small but significant minority who believed the answer to this question was no, the majority of librarians, and indeed the public at large, accepted that the only realistic response was yes. This then raised the far more complex question of what types of novels should be provided. At one end of the spectrum was the opinion that libraries, as publicly funded institutions, should reflect public demand and supply as much popular fiction as was necessary to meet this. As Edward Edwards noted of Manchester's library committee, its aim was to provide 'the most general provision of literature consistent with pure taste and a moral tone; – the province of a public representative body seeming to be that of providing liberally for all proper demands, while refraining from all restrictions not absolutely imperative'.[1] At the other extreme was a more restrictive approach under which popular fiction was to be virtually excluded, and only standard English novels were to be bought. In between these two positions were a variety of approaches which combined elements of both schools of opinion, prepared to supply some popular fiction but hoping to educate readers to progress to better things. Many librarians were simply resigned to the predominant demand for fiction, sometimes expressing their predicament with wry humour (see Appendix).

The Great Fiction Question was partly an outcome of the prevailing social concerns about literature and reading of the later nineteenth and early twentieth centuries, and these have already been discussed. However, aspects of public library practice and of the evolution of the library profession also contributed to the provision of fiction becoming *the* major issue in librarianship. These included the working-class base of public library fiction readership, the practice of book selection by committee, the accusations that fiction provision was a misuse of the rates and the undermining of the professional status of librarians and of the image of the public library caused by the dominance of fiction borrowing. Finally, the introduction of open access in 1893, when borrowers were able for the first time to choose their books from the shelf as opposed to a printed catalogue, raised worries about readers' abilities to choose books wisely, and fundamentally changed the role of the librarian from that of custodian of books to that of an adviser and guide in reading. As this particular concern was related directly to the users of libraries, it is useful to start with a brief analysis of the readership of public library fiction.

The readership of public library fiction

The preceding chapters have described the ways in which attitudes to popular fiction were influenced by the socio-economic status of the reader, and this was particularly relevant to public libraries as their borrowers were drawn mainly from the working and lower middle classes.

In the early days of public libraries, middle-class readers could afford the fees charged by commercial subscription libraries from which new books could be procured more quickly than from public libraries;[2] for working-class readers, such fees, for example, the ten shillings and sixpence per annum at Stirling's Public Library in Glasgow, were prohibitive.[3] Public libraries may not have regarded themselves as being in competition with commercial libraries such as Mudie's and Smith's, but they did hope to draw custom away from the small and cheap circulating libraries which supplied, primarily to working-class customers, romances, fashionable novels and what Webb refers to as 'books decidedly bad'.[4] It would be incorrect to imply that middle-class readers did not borrow novels from public libraries; indeed, at the turn of the century, one writer accused public libraries of providing middle-class borrowers with the latest sensation novels.[5] Nevertheless, as Kelly has shown, there is overwhelming evidence that the majority of users of public libraries were working class,[6] and this can be clearly seen in annual reports and in the parliamentary returns of public libraries.[7] Edward Edwards noted in his first annual report at Manchester that ' . . . the majority of evening readers – and it is in the evening that the library is most largely frequented – have always belonged to what are properly termed the working class';[8] another observer in the 1870s also reported that their readers were drawn from 'all classes, but chiefly the working classes'.[9] At Manchester's Ancoats branch library, the membership included 536 artisans and mechanics, 238 cotton factory workers, 123 clerks and salesmen, 180 warehousemen and 621 persons 'entirely undescribed of whom probably a majority are women and children'; there were, however, only five artists and designers, four clergymen and professional men and nine merchants. By the turn of the century, the pattern of working- and lower middle-class predominance was almost universal; the proportions of the occupations of borrowers registered at Accrington public library in 1901 (see Table 4.1) would not be untypical of most urban public libraries.[10]

Table 4.1 Occupations of borrowers registered at Acrrington library in 1901

Scholars (i.e. juveniles)	749
Weavers	460
Clerks	192
Teachers	137
Labourers	126
Fitters	69
Dressmakers	49

Even though public libraries were for everybody, it was generally felt, especially by librarians, that they were intended primarily for working-class readers. Librarians welcomed this and saw in it a moral imperative to work for the improvement of popular reading habits. The impression of a missionary undertaking to the vast masses of ill-educated and unsophisticated working-class populations is inescapable in reading the professional press of the period. Sensation novels, cheap newspapers and magazines and the new commercial leisure attractions all made the task of the librarian more difficult, and, as one noted:

> The fact is, few of the working-class have either the time or the inclination for a course of serious reading. They are therefore the more eager to spend the spare time at their disposal in the quest of recreation and amusement. Further, there are so many places of amusement open now, as compared with a decade or two ago, that their attractions are multiplied by reason of their cheapness. Studying such resorts and their patrons, we find ourselves again brought into contact with the baneful influence which is so surely sapping away the strength and character of our press. Week by week we

find the second-rate theatres filling their bills with dramas, in which impossible incidents, with lurid sentimental effects, are the climax to every act in the plays depicted.

To effect a change, we must first endeavour to alter the material surroundings of the classes concerned ere we may hope to see the library taking its proper position amongst the educational elements of the country. Thus, on every hand, we find the tendencies of public taste are in opposition to the idea of the library being the direct means of stopping of removing the evil. Daily we are reminded that Scott and other standard authors are out of favour – if not out-of-date, because to express it in a popular phrase, they are too dry. In other words they do not yield that amount of sensational reading which a work of Guy Boothby or Miss Braddon affords to their patrons'.[11]

The use of public libraries by working-class readers may have discouraged some middle-class readers from visiting them; a speaker at the Library Association's 1881 conference described how in one library which was frequented by a 'mixed class of readers' it had been necessary to issue fiction and light reading from one room and 'higher and more recondite' subjects from another room to protect middle-class readers from the working-class crowds.[12]

To state that working-class readers formed the bulk of public library users is a broad generalization, and there were finer distinctions. Among the more significant of these is the fact that fiction borrowers often tended to be female, a point noted by Peter Cowell, the librarian at Liverpool.[13] This links libraries with the expansion of the market for fiction from the mid-nineteenth century onwards, which was in large part based upon women readers, initially middle-class women who were not employed and therefore had ample time for reading, but, later on, women from all social classes. There was a convention that women should be protected from certain types of fiction, as they were, in the opinion of one critic, 'always impressionable' and easily influenced by novels![14] Much of the concern about popular reading was specifically about women's reading – the 'shop-girls, seamstresses and domestic servants' who read the penny novelettes and poorer sorts of sensation story.[15] It seems that initially women often found public libraries to be unwelcoming, possibly because most of the staff were male and possibly because ladies' rooms did not become not common until the 1880s.[16] One lady, writing of the Manchester branch libraries in 1870, complained that they were oppressive, though she did note that women who did use these libraries borrowed mainly fiction.[17] A similar criticism of libraries appeared in *All the year round* in 1892, this time with reference to Bermondsey public library which, it was stated, tended to be unattractive to the working-class women of its catchment area, whereas the Hammersmith and Kensington public library, located in a wealthier area, was well used by women of a 'superior cast' for obtaining novels and fashion magazines.[18] By the 1890s public libraries were certainly well patronized by women, principally for obtaining fiction, and received much disparaging criticism in contemporary newspapers on account of this.

In contrast to these paternalistic attitudes to women's reading was a more realistic and pragmatic approach, exemplified in the comment of a librarian employed in Birmingham's public library: 'The women of the working class are, however, in this respect little worse than women of other classes. Nearly all women read fiction, little else but fiction, and if they ceased to read that, they would read nothing at all'.[19] Thomas Greenwood, too, noted that women read mainly fiction, and saw nothing amiss in this:

> Women who are practically domestic drudges and have no variety in life save the occasional episode of new babies, who from one year's end to another are engaged in an endless turmoil of dish-washing, floor-scrubbing, clothes-washing, bed-making, clothes-mending and general house cleaning duties are just the very class to whom the novel comes as absolutely the sole intellectual amusement. There are thousands of such women in every large town, and it is they who read more than one-half of the novels which are circulated by Public Libraries. And he is a boor who would deny them such a cheap, helpful and stimulating pleasure. Far from being critical and censorious, we ought to be thankful that working women find solace and forget the steam of the wash tub in following the heroines of Miss Braddon, Mrs. Wood, Miss Yonge, Mrs. Worboise, Edna Lyall, Rosa Carey and others, though their varied experiences. Of what earthly use to such women are the works of Mr. Herbert Spencer or the late Adam Smith?[20]

Although views of this kind were not found everywhere, many librarians nevertheless shared them. James Duff Brown spoke of the futility of trying to persuade women to read what were usually referred to as classic novels when they much preferred the stories of everyday life as written by Rosa Carey, Emma Worboise and Mrs Henry Wood:

> The great majority of Public Library novel-readers are women, and it is impossible to get many of them to read authors like Tennyson, Balzac, Scott, Thackeray, Cooper and others of an even lower literary standard. They want novels of every-day life, written for women by women, in which story completely overshadows style, educational intention and even conventional morality . . .
>
> The day has not yet come when the shop-girl who can read is going to be

fobbed off with Sidney's Arcadia, Peacock's Melincourt or Howell's Silas Lapham when she wants and can only understand writers like Carey, Wood, Emma Jane Worboise and more modern clean sensationalists like Oppenheim, Tracy, White, Oxenham, Marchmont and all the rest of them.[21]

Sometimes, attitudes to women's fiction borrowing could be quite liberal by contemporary standards, and the provision of fiction for relaxation and recuperation was seen as a valid public library function; as William McGill of Islington public library commented: 'A Library in a mill town issuing 80 per cent. of good fiction circulating in the homes of tired working women may be doing as good work as one issuing 40 per cent. in a more cultured community'.[22] Despite such affirmations, prejudice against women's reading flourished, and one newspaper went so far as to remind its female readers that novel reading should not be allowed to interrupt their household duties.[23]

A further relevant aspect of public library memberships is that young readers formed a substantial proportion of them – for instance, 56% of Birmingham's members were under 20 years of age. The publishing industry produced a steady flow of penny dreadfuls and other sensational publications for this market and libraries felt they had a moral obligation to provide some countermeasure. Librarians and committees with any degree of pragmatism realized that younger readers were as unlikely to be attracted by solid works and worthy tomes as were their parents. As the chairman of Birmingham's library committee said, most people acquired the reading habit through exposure to novels and tales when young, and libraries had little alternative to providing lighter recreational publications if they were to have any success in appealing to the younger adults.[24]

Book selection principles and practices

During their first five years, public libraries had to rely on donations for their stock, as the 1850 Act did not allow them to buy books. As a result, many acquired collections of second-hand books and a wide range of fiction and recreational material. The 1855 Act permitted expenditure on the book stock, and the practice of book selection became a major element of the fiction question. The task of purchasing public library stock was a jealously guarded privilege, and while there was a consensus that obscene novels or those of an extremely poor literary standard should not be purchased, each library was free to act as it saw fit in the selection of fiction. In keeping with contemporary values in recreation, morality was a key factor, and as a report on early public libraries commented 'everywhere supervision is exercised by the librarian and the committee in order to keep out what is immoral, or of a low sensational character'.[25] The question of what was provided, and perhaps more significantly of what was not, placed pressure on librarians who were widely regarded as arbiters of public morality, sometimes unfairly, as it was usually the library committee rather than the librarian which had the final say in book selection. Nevertheless, when public libraries were accused by critics, as they often were, of buying immoral books, it was the librarian who was the first to be called upon to defend the service, and this probably contributed to the impression that librarians were responsible for selecting the books.

The professional press published innumerable articles on the principles and methods of choosing books for public libraries, yet of all the aspects of librarianship which might have laid claim to be a core element of professional autonomy, none remained under closer municipal control than book selection. This was usually effected through the machinery of a book selection sub-committee of the library committee for which the librarian was, in some authorities, allowed to compile a list of recommended purchases, although in others he was not involved in the selection process at all. The librarian at Lambeth recorded how he presented lists to the selection committee based on a perusal of the book reviews in the highbrow journals – the *Athenaeum*, *Literary world* and *Saturday review* – and this practice doubtlessly occurred in other libraries.[26] Selection by committee was the standard practice in pre-1914 public libraries and indeed for many decades after this. It was only after the Second World War that the responsibility for choosing the books to be purchased was delegated to professional librarians, although in at least one library authority, Darwen in Lancashire, the anachronism of selection by committee persisted until local government reorganization in 1974.

Book selection committees

The practice of book selection by committee connected the treatment of fiction in public libraries to external factors. The criteria used in the selection process depended in a large part upon the composition of the library committee and its book selection sub-committee. Book selection sub-committee members had differing motives in their selection of books, and a library's purchasing policy reflected, in varying degrees, the political, religious and cultural values of the library committee. Book selection, and public library practice in its entirety, were not, as is sometimes implied, simply an outcome of professional idealism and training, although these were certainly of some influence, but a product of a complex interaction between public demand, library committees and the values they represented.

Like membership of the library committee, that of the book selection sub-committee was not restricted to elected councillors, as it was permissible to coopt anyone to it; ideally, someone whose literary knowledge would be helpful in choosing books. Coopted members were usually drawn from the middle classes and were, as Hanson described them, 'gentlemen of literary ability and taste, who are not connected with the Council'.[27] However coopted members were not always chosen on this basis, for in some towns they included local representatives of all religious denominations irrespective of literary knowledge, while in other places coopted members were invited primarily for political or social patronage. Librarians sometimes attended book selection meetings but, as Greenwood observed, were often compelled to be speechless, only answering questions if asked.[28] This led Stanley Jast to observe that it was difficult to decide whether the ideal book selection committee members were those who were knowledgeable about books or ignorant of them, as the former were difficult to deal with, while the latter, although they might possess little literary expertise, were more likely to depend on the knowledge of the librarian, and to be guided by him when purchasing books.[29]

Book selection committees were powerful and could readily ignore the advice of librarians, and selection practice was thus frequently a source of conflict between the librarian and his committee. This would typically be so where a librarian wished to use literary merit as a criterion in fiction selection but was obliged to give way to a committee eager to provide large stocks of popular novels. The resulting tension between librarians and selection committees provoked numerous articles and letters in the professional press of the period and was in fact discussed at the Library Association conference in 1900, where it was noted that not only did committee members frequently disagree among themselves on questions of book purchase, but that many of them knew little about books in the first place.[30] James Duff Brown was scathing in his criticism of selection committees, claiming that 'Nothing comes amiss to these cocksure local notables and it is only fair to say that, in most cases of abject failure, it is the interference of zealous ignorance which is the prime cause', and illustrated his point with an account of how in one public library authority the committee had allegedly driven round the town to visit second-hand booksellers to buy books in bulk with the single aim of filling the library's shelves.[31] Ernest Baker also held book selection committees in low esteem and criticized their tendency to be over-impressed by cheap books: 'There are public libraries that I know which have for years been stocked with the sweepings of Mudies' and other libraries, bought at a price that was meant to stagger committee men, and which now challenge any circulating library in the world to compete with them in the supply of the largest numbers of the worst novels published'.[32] However, three-decker novels were not generally liked by librarians, for, as Greenwood noted, they were expensive to buy, expensive to rebind, occupied a lot of shelf space, and were a source of endless trouble to issue.[33]

An article in the *Westminster review* in 1906[34] complained that literary knowledge and cultural taste were usually the last criteria in appointing men to book selection committees, as the aim was normally to ensure that the committee was representative of everything *except* literature; it was also common that when someone on the committee did happen to be knowledgeable about books, the rest of the committee were reluctant to be seen to rely too heavily on one person's opinion. Book selection committees could thus help librarians to develop a bookstock of literary excellence or could frustrate them by purchasing in bulk novels about which they knew or cared little simply to fill the shelves and increase the issues. This exposed libraries to criticisms of being too leisure-orientated, and caused resentment among librarians, who found such accusations damaging to their attempts to gain acceptance as a profession.

Librarians and book selection

The best that most librarians could hope for was an advisory role in book selection, in which they could steer a course between the unquestioning supply of popular novels to meet demand and the purchase of novels on literary merit. This was not an easy task, for librarians were not best placed to challenge selection committee decisions: the committees were, after all, their employers.[35] Deprived of real power, librarians could do little other than develop principles and theories of book selection in the hope that committees might be persuaded to use these, and many articles and letters were devoted to discussing which kinds of books libraries ought to buy. Daniel Herdman, Sunderland's deputy librarian, thought that although the primary objective of public libraries was to spread knowledge, this did not necessarily exclude fiction. Fiction was, he said, an interpreter of life which promoted a 'common understanding between the higher and lower classes of society' and because many novels had great educational potential, these should be purchased and cross-referenced in the subject index, especially when they dealt with a topic of educational importance, such as history or geography.[36] Ernest Baker also believed that education was the primary function of the public library, and that therefore the only novels a library should buy were those which had either a practical educational purpose or which had an 'emotional and spiritual bearing on our lives'.[37] Some critics would not even allow this; 'no novel', one writer noted, 'reaches the demand for a good work of history, travel or philosophy. Professor Drummond's *Natural law in the spiritual world* has left all fiction far behind'.[38]

A further selection technique was not to purchase new fiction until a period of time had elapsed. At one stage, Manchester public library stopped buying fiction under two years old unless there was a special reason for doing otherwise.[39] In a paper delivered to the Library Assistants' Association in 1913, Mr R. Parr, the Local Government Board Auditor, suggested that where there might be pressure from ratepayers to spend the library budget in accordance with their views, that is not to provide 'inferior' or 'objectionable' works, there should be a three-year delay between the publication of novel and its purchase as a public library stock item, as 'three fourths of the novels that appear have by that time ceased to be read'.[40] There was a danger in this strategy, if it were pursued too vigorously, that libraries would contain so few popular novels that the public would simply cease to use them. Many librarians seem to have been either unaware of or unconcerned by this, even though Berwick Sayers, sub-librarian at Croydon, warned them about it on a number of occasions,[41, 42] and developed ingenious arguments for further reductions in fiction purchases. Ernest Savage,[43] for example, noted that although fiction represented 70% of the issue, it should not form a similar proportion of the total stock because as only 10–12% of a town's population normally used the library, the demands of such a small proportion should not determine what books the library should provide.

THE INTRODUCTION OF OPEN ACCESS

Of the several factors which contributed to the crisis presented by the Great Fiction Question, few were more significant than the introduction of open access in public library lending departments. Allowing borrowers to choose their books directly from the shelves marked the single biggest change in public library practice since their introduction. Open access enabled users to handle the books on the shelves and, by enhancing their choice, provided a more positive leisure experience. It also fundamentally changed the nature of the librarian's role from custodial to advisory, and stimulated debate on guidance and advice as an aspect of professional autonomy.

Before open access, readers could not browse the shelves in lending departments, although a small number of libraries offered such a facility in their reference departments. Instead, they chose their books from a printed catalogue and made a request at a counter from which an assistant would retrieve the books, which were normally identified by an accession number. One library historian recalled the method of borrowing a book from a public library as being similar to approaching a railway ticket office '. . . at which a borrower handed in a slip with a list of the books wanted. With this in hand the assistant went to the shelves, and, if the borrower was lucky, he might be given one or other of the books asked for; if not, his slip was handed back to him with the laconic remark, "All out" '.[44] Most libraries eventually provided some type of indicator which showed if a book was in the library or on loan as a means of reducing the number of requests which could not be satisfied, but the reader still had to obtain his or her book through the intermediary assistance of a member of the library staff.

The revolutionary practice of allowing library users direct access to the shelves was introduced in Great Britain by James Duff Brown at Clerkenwell in 1893; Bournemouth was the second public library to implement open access; Darwen, in Lancashire followed in 1895,[45] until, by 1901, approximately 30 public libraries had adopted the system.[46] Brown described his reason for implementing open access as mainly one of convenience for borrowers, claiming that the then current procedures for borrowing made the selection of books a 'heartbreak and a labour tinctured with disgust'.[47] Open access was technically defined as:

> The system of allowing readers in a library direct, free, or open access to the shelves, thus enabling them to handle books before selecting them. Safeguarded open access is the system whereby borrowers or readers before entering to choose books must show their ticket, or sign their name etc. in a book provided for the purpose and in which close classification and other safeguards are employed.[48]

Initially, open access received a hostile reception. When Blackpool public library undertook a questionnaire survey of librarians' attitudes to open access, it received 115 negative responses out of a total of 143,[49] and Berwick Sayers later claimed that 90% of the library profession were actively antagonistic to it.[50] The reasons for this were complex. One of the main objections was the understandable fear of theft, and it is true that some libraries which adopted the system reported a number of losses, although none of these appears to have been of drastic proportions. A more significant objection was that open access would encourage an increase in fiction borrowing. This was based upon a distrust of the public and a suspicion that readers were not competent to use an open access library intelligently, and would be immediately drawn to bright and attractively bound fiction. One librarian felt that the average reader had very little idea of the workings of a library subject-classification system, and that when this confusion was exacerbated by the misplacing of books upon the shelves by other browsers, the reader would inevitably drift into the reading of fiction 'out of sheer disgust'.[51] It was predicted that users would head for the fiction shelves, find novels by authors of whom they had not previously heard, neglect standard fiction and gravitate towards sensation and adventure novels. Kensington library, for example, declined to adopt open access because it was felt that it would bewilder the non-purposeful borrower and distract serious information seekers from the newsroom to the lending department, where they would fritter time away in aimless browsing.[52] This fear of an 'aimless' use of public libraries, in which borrowers would choose books in a random, leisure-orientated manner, was the basis of numerous articles and letters in the professional press. Again, attitudes to open access were influenced by considerations of the social status of the reader, one librarian stating that open access had some points in its favour with reference to the 'better class of persons' who would take care of the books and replace them carefully, but with the 'ordinary' class of borrowers, '70 or 80 per cent of whom would come for recreation or pastime, the system is not required, while the wear and tear on the books would be enormously increased'.[53] In addition, this writer noted, the influx of fiction readers would so crowd the shelves as to cause severe inconvenience to 'serious' borrowers. Because of this, some libraries allowed open access to the non-fiction shelves while retaining closed access to fiction, while others interspersed fiction shelves among non-fiction shelves, partly to relieve overcrowding and partly in the hope that readers in search of fiction might come across an appealing volume of non-fiction and borrow this instead. A further argument against open access to fiction was that borrowers would hide desirable novels in other parts of the library in order to collect them at a later date.

The development of guidance and advisory work in fiction

The immediate effect of open access upon the library profession was the growth of an awareness of the need to provide readers with assistance in their use of libraries. Ernest Baker likened the uneducated reader in the public library to a boy 'plumped down among the laboratories and apparatus of a great college, and a college where there are no lecturers to guide his footsteps. More melancholy still is it to see hundreds of thousands dissipating their intellectual energies on trash because the road into the true world of literature has never been pointed out'.[54] As borrowers no longer had to consult catalogues from which to make specific requests, the role of the librarian changed to one of providing advice and guidance to borrowers in their choice of books. In the case of non-fiction titles, this was fairly easily accomplished by developing classification systems and subject catalogues. Fiction, however, could not easily be dealt with in this manner.

Although interest in the provision of guidance and advisory work was increased by the introduction of open access, it did not originate in it. In 1887, Birmingham library had experimented with library lectures on books, with a view to directing the attention of readers to the books they should read for any particular study.[55] However, open access turned guidance and advice into major elements of the library service, and the change in the role of the librarian from custodian to adviser received extensive discussion in national and local newspapers. The need for guidance brought about through open access coincided with a general recognition that the expansion in publishing output was confusing to many readers who would appreciate some advice and direction in charting a course through the mass output of the book trade. As Greenwood noted:

> Everyone has probably heard of some little society of young ladies who undertake to spend a certain time each day in the perusal of a literary classic. These little groups of people are a very general symptom of a want which is widely felt of some direction, some advice, and superintendence of the efforts which so many are eager to make for self-instruction.[56]

An article on the increase in the number of newly published books and the expanding literary market, which appeared in the *Manchester Evening Chronicle* in 1903, echoed a widely held concern about a lowering of standards: 'In this age of multifarious publications many people have forgotten how to read, and certainly cannot tell what to read . . . The great need of the age now is guidance and restraint'.[57] It was exactly such a role in 'guidance and restraint' that appealed to librarians, as borrowers were increasingly being given free access to popular novels and tales in lending departments. There was a considerable degree of public support for librarians undertaking this role; the *Manchester Guardian*, for instance, welcomed the fact that open access had changed their role to that of adviser,[58] while the *Southport Visitor* recognized that librarians had an important position as gatekeepers who would offer advice on the worth of a book.[59] This was widely accepted elsewhere, albeit sometimes with a note of caution similar to that expressed by the *Northern Daily Telegraph*: 'If these public functionaries are to be encouraged to recommend books, it should be clearly understood and enforced that their advice should be confined to literary considerations and should not extend to opinions'.[60]

Librarians developed their role as adviser and guide around the two pillars of literary standards and systematic reading. Systematic reading embodied Victorian ideals of recreation – it was utilitarian, improving and morally uplifting, whereas casual reading was simply aimless amusement. Wright, the librarian at Accrington, described systematic reading as being based upon considerations of careful, critical and discriminating reading with purpose; in the context of fiction, this required attention to plot, characterization, literary quality and moral teaching.[61]

Systematic reading

Systematic reading was seen to be needed for a number of reasons, most of which were connected to a fear of declining literary standards in an age of increased commercial publishing and a growth in the mass reading public. In the discussion of guidance and advisory work in the professional library press of the late nineteenth and early twentieth centuries, there is a widely encountered notion of the uneducated working-class reader as an ignorant layman in the new world of open-access literature, prey to the distractions of non-improving novels of low literary merit. Literary critics believed that more meant worse, and some even blamed public libraries for what they perceived as a national decline in the standard of reading. Libraries were comprehensively attacked by John Churton Collins, Professor of English Literature at the University of Birmingham, in a paper in the *Nineteenth century* in 1903 titled 'Free libraries: their functions and opportunities',[62] in which he accused public libraries of encouraging reading which simply passed the time in idle amusement, as many libraries were 'completely under the thraldom of those who only seek such recreation as shilling shockers, newspapers and the ordinary comic rags afford that they cannot be regarded as unmixed evils'. Churton Collins believed that librarians ought to stock fiction that was 'at least, wholesome and of merit or distinction', and to this end they had a duty to ensure that the literature provided was excellent rather than mediocre. He also wrote that they had a further responsibility to enable readers to use libraries intelligently and with discrimination. It is relevant that a sound knowledge and appreciation of English literature were considered to be essential attributes in the aspiring professional librarian, and this was accordingly tested in professional examinations. These included challenging and difficult papers on literary history; for example, the 1905 paper included questions on 'The imaginative writers of Australia' and 'The essays of Addison', the 1907 paper on 'Charles Lamb' and 'A comparison between English literature at the beginning and end of the nineteenth century'.

The work of Ernest Baker

Guidance and advisory work in fiction assumed a variety of forms. Many initiatives were developed at a local level, with the better practices being copied or adapted by other libraries. These included the production of annotated catalogues, lists of recommended fiction, and library magazines. On a national basis, the work of Ernest Baker, who became a recognized authority on the provision of fiction in public libraries between the turn of the century and the First World War, was of immense influence. Baker was born in 1869 in Bath, gained an external BA from the University of London, and was appointed in 1893 as librarian of the Midland Railway Institute in Derby, where he quickly became well-known through his numerous contributions to the professional press. In 1904, he entered public library work, when he was appointed chief librarian of Wallasey public libraries, later becoming the borough librarian of Woolwich in 1906 and gaining the external degree of

DLitt from the University of London. In 1912, he left public library employment to undertake literary and publishing work, although he remained an active member of The Library Association. He was for several years the examiner for the Association's Literary History paper.

Baker was deeply interested in fiction provision in public libraries. In 1900, he published an article in the *Library Association record*,[63] in which he argued that the demand for fiction, which until then had been generally harmful to the public library's image, could be used to advantage by librarians if it were turned into a basis upon which to develop systematic approaches to reading. He commented specifically upon the need for a guide to novels which would help librarians to advise readers choosing fiction, and, in a later article, suggested that librarians should produce annotated lists of novels to promote the reading of good fiction and to encourage the use of educational novels in courses of study.[64] In 1903 Baker published his *Descriptive guide to the best fiction*,[65] prepared with the help of James Duff Brown, which had the objective of providing 'a fairly complete list of the best prose fiction in English, including not all that interests students, but all that the ordinary reader is likely to come about, with as much description of matter and style for the guidance of readers, as can be condensed into a few lines of print for each book'. Although the *Guide* was not written expressly for librarians, Baker was aware of the furore provoked by open access and the demand for fiction, and realized that it would be a useful tool to them. He adopted a catholic and sometimes idiosyncratic approach to his selection of the best fiction; novelists of whom he was later to write disparagingly, among them Mary Braddon, Mrs Henry Wood and Ouida, were included. Even Guy Boothby featured, being described as a 'crude and popular author', who 'aims at sensation pure and simple, and gathers his material from every source; gigantic adventures, gory monsters and supernatural beings are as common as ordinary men of the world'. In 1906, he published a further article in the *Contemporary review*,[66] which restated the need to provide guidance to library readers, noting that '. . . to manufacture readers by means of Education Acts, and to establish free libraries in every big town, [implies] some obligation to furnish means of guidance'. His frequent contributions to professional journals ensured wide publicity for his views.

Library magazines

Many local initiatives originated in Baker's ideas, particularly the production of annotated lists of novels. From such lists, public library readers' magazines evolved as a method of promoting the reading of worthwhile books. These magazines enjoyed a vogue in the years immediately preceding the First World War, and many libraries produced one. Examples include

Manchester's *Libraries quarterly review*, Kingston-upon-Thames' *Our new books*, Leeds' *Public library quarterly journal* and Bootle's *Library journal*. These magazines were modestly priced or free, and contained miscellaneous short pieces of literary interest. The *Chorley library journal*, for example, was published quarterly and edited by Edward McKnight, the Borough Librarian. Priced one penny, the *Journal* included potted biographies of local worthies, reports and reviews of library lectures, articles on local history and, as a major objective of the *Journal* was to encourage interest in works other than popular novels, lists of recommended books.

At Accrington, where the library was opened with the open access system installed, the first issue of the *Accrington public library quarterly journal* confirmed the librarian's view that such a publication would be worthwhile and would popularize the library when, of the 500 copies printed, 400 were sold at one penny each within a few weeks.[67]

Library magazines were often self-financing through advertising revenue and cover charges, and offered a cheap and effective means of encouraging library borrowers to read books other than popular novels. Many enjoyed a reasonable longevity; Accrington's *Journal*, for example, survived in its original format until 1908 when, like many similar publications, it was replaced by the National Home Reading Union's *Readers' review*.

Fiction classification

The aim of providing guidance also created an interest in the classification of fiction, with Ernest Baker once again being a major influence. Baker published a series of articles in the *Library world* in 1898 and 1899, in which he proposed that a classification of fiction would encourage readers to sample works other than those by already-known novelists:

> a large and familiar class of readers, and very intelligent too, many of them, are coyly reluctant to venture on an unknown author, no matter how you encourage them; and they spend a lifetime in studying and collating the valuable tomes of Ouida and Miss Braddon. If representative samples of the regular novel-readers were examined, it would surprise us to learn within what narrow limits most of them find their enjoyment. What proportion, do you think, have ever read a review in their lives? John Ruskin's indictment of excessive and unintelligent reading, if ever true, must be true here. But an intelligible sorting-out of novels into groups and classes will give the reader a series of advantages. Foremost of these, he will learn what are the best works.[68]

He suggested that novels could be categorized in terms of time, place and nationality, but conceded that this system would be somewhat basic and would need careful annotation to be effective. The concept of classifying fiction reflected a widely held view within the profession that, at its best, fiction *was* education, but those who shared this opinion would have done well to recall Edward Edwards' basic observation that novel reading was, in the main, undertaken for recreation, not intellectual growth.[69] James Duff Brown was sceptical about fiction classification, partly because, like all selective annotated lists, this scheme would draw attention to the books excluded from it, and would label 'in the most unmistakable manner the very class of fiction which every librarian believes should be kept away from the general and young reader'.[70]

The Great Fiction Question presented librarians with an insoluble dilemma. If libraries refused to buy fiction, or restricted fiction to novels of literary merit, their popular appeal would be immediately diminished and their rate of use would fall; furthermore, librarians would be accused of assuming the mantle of public censor. If, on the other hand, they provided popular fiction in response to demand, they were accused of neglecting their educational objectives, misusing ratepayers' money, and failing to take a lead in developing the reading habit. To make matters worse, librarians themselves were not in full control of the situation, as they were seldom in a position to control purchasing policies and, instead, had to follow and implement the decisions made by their governing committees. The key questions were as follows: how did individual libraries respond to the issue of whether to provide fiction or a particular type of fiction, and what caused one library to behave differently to another? To provide some answers to these questions, the next three chapters analyse the three broad responses to the fiction question: not to provide fiction at all; to provide some fiction only, and to provide as much fiction as possible in response to popular demand.

NOTES AND REFERENCES TO CHAPTER 4

1   Edwards, E., *Free town libraries*, Trubner, 1869, 143.
2   Johnman, W. A. P and Kendall, M., *Report of the commission appointed to inquire into the condition and working of Free Libraries in various towns in England*, Darlington Philanthropic Society, 1869.
3   *Report to the annual meeting of subscribers*, Stirling Public Library, Glasgow, 1864.
4   Webb, R. K., 'The Victorian reading public', in *Pelican guide to English literature. Volume 6*, Penguin, 1958, 205-26.
5   '"Working Woman", Do public libraries foster a love of literature among the masses?', *Chamber's journal*, series 6, 3, 1899, 134-6.
6   Kelly, T., *A history of public libraries in Great Britain 1845–1975*, Library Association, 1977, 81-4.

7   Great Britain, House of Commons, *Further returns relating to the Free Libraries Acts*, 1877, [277].

8   Credland, W. R., *The Manchester public free libraries*, The Public Free Libraries Committee of Manchester, 1899.

9   Hanson, J., Free public libraries, *Westminster review*, **98**, October 1872, 333–77.

10   Borough of Accrington, *First annual report of the free library*, 1901–1902.

11   Gordon, P. D., 'Open access', *Library assistant*, **2**, 1899, 137–43.

12   Archer, W., 'Suggestions as to public library buildings', *Transactions and proceedings of the 4th annual meeting of The Library Association, 1881*.

13   Cowell, P., 'On the admission of fiction in free public libraries', in *Transactions and proceedings of the Conference of Librarians held in London*, 1877, 44–5.

14   Gregg, W. R., 'False morality of lady novelists', *National review*, **8**, 1859, 144–67.

15   See for instance: Salmon, Edward G., 'What the working classes read', *Nineteenth century*, **20**, 1886, 108–17; Leigh, John Garnett, 'What do the masses read?', *Economic review*, **14** (2), 1904, 166–77.

16   Kelly, op. cit., ref. 6, 68.

17   Mrs. Lord, *Why do not women make greater use of the Free Libraries?* Manchester, Heywood, 1870.

18   'A day at the London Free Libraries', *All the year round*, **26**, March 1892, 305–9.

19   Grindle, H., 'The fiction question', *Library assistant*, January 1912, 6–16.

20   Greenwood, T., 'The great fiction question', *Library year book*, Cassell, 1897, 107–16.

21   Brown, J. Duff, 'In defence of Emma Jane', *Library world*, **3**, 1900–1901, 215–19.

22   McGill, W., 'Library statistics necessary and unnecessary and the purpose of statistics', *Library assistant*, **160**, May 1911, 84–92.

23   *Northern Daily Telegraph*, 13 September 1906.

24   President's address to The Library Association, 1887.

25   Johnman and Kendall, op. cit., ref. 2.

26   Burgoyne, F., 'The selection and purchase of books', *Library world*, **1**, 1898, 136–8.

27   Hanson, op. cit., ref. 9.

28   Greenwood, T., *Public libraries*, Cassell, 4th edn, 1894, 353.

29   Jast, L. S., 'Committee work', *Library assistant*, **73**, January 1904, 42–5.

30   *Library Association record*, 1900, 529–33.

31   Brown, J. D., *The small library: a guide to the collection and care of books*, Routledge, 1907.

32   Baker, E., 'Standard of fiction in public libraries', *Library Association record*, 1907, 70–80.
33   Greenwood, op. cit., ref. 28, 401–2.
34   Hardman, W. M., 'Free libraries and fiction', *Westminster review*, February 1906, 209–15.
35   See: Baker, E. A., op. cit., ref. 32.
36   Herdman, D. W., 'The place and treatment of fiction in public libraries', *Library assistant*, **138**, July 1909, 375–82.
37   Baker, E.A., 'Book selection: some fundamental principles and some applications', *Library Association record*, 1911, 17–29.
38   Gilburt, J., 'Library surplusage', *Library chronicle*, **2**, 1885, 90–3.
39   Grindle, op. cit., ref. 19.
40   Parr, R. T. L., 'The public library movement from the rate payers' point of view', *Library assistant*, **192**, January 1914, 4–13.
41   Sayers, W. B., 'The decline in the reading of fiction', *Library world*, **12**, 1909–1910, 453–5.
42   Sayers, W. B., 'The place of fiction today in libraries', *Library Association record*, 1914, 273–9.
43   Savage, E., 'Book selection', *Library assistant*, **84**, December 1904, 190–5.
44   Minto, J., *A history of the public library movement in Great Britain and Ireland*, Allen and Unwin, 1932, 152.
45   Kelly, op. cit., ref. 6, 176–9.
46   'Two reports on open access', *Library world*, 1901, 116–21.
47   Brown, J. D., 'A plea for liberty to readers to help themselves', *Library*, **4**, 1892, 302–5.
48   *Library world*, May 1907–1908, 438.
49   *Blackpool Herald and Fylde Advertiser*, 7 December 1900.
50   Kelly, op. cit., ref 6, 179.
51   *Municipal journal*, 29 November 1901, 91.
52   ibid.
53   'Two reports on open access', op. cit., ref. 46.
54   Baker, E. A., 'Direction for popular readers', *Contemporary review*, April 1906, 498–504.
55   'President's address to the Library Association Conference', *Library chronicle*, **4**, 1887, 129–35.
56   Greenwood, op. cit., ref. 28, 421.
57   *Manchester Evening Chronicle*, 3 April 1903.
58   *Manchester Guardian*, 9 February 1903.
59   *Southport Visitor*, 25 August 1898.
60   *Northern Daily Telegraph*, 30 September 1907.
61   Wright, C., 'The public library, iv, Systematic reading', *Accrington*

Observer, 4 May 1901.

62 Collins, J. C., 'Free libraries: their functions and opportunities', *Nineteenth century*, June 1903, 968–81.

63 Baker, E. A., 'Wanted – a guide-book to books', *Library Association record*, **2**, 1900, 89–97.

64 Baker, E. A., 'The fiction nuisance and its abatement: a sequel', *Library world*, **5**, March 1903, 225–7.

65 Baker, E. A., *A descriptive guide to the best fiction: British and American*, London, Swan Sonnenschein, 1903.

66 Baker, E. A., 'Direction for popular readers', *Contemporary review*, April 1906, 498–504.

67 Borough of Accrington, *Minutes of the meeting of the library committee 19 June 1902*.

68 Baker, E. A., 'The classification of fiction', *Library world*, 1898–1900, 198–201 and 216–20.

69 Edwards, op. cit., ref. 1, 79.

70 Brown, J. D., 'The annotation of fiction', *Library world*, **2**, 1899–1900, 150–4.

Chapter 5
The Anti-Fiction Campaign

A longside the general acceptance of the provision of recreational reading and other leisure-related services as a core function of the public library, there has always been a small but vocal minority who have argued that libraries should provide only education and information services. This was particularly so before the First World War, when fiction provision received a critical bombardment from sources both within and beyond the library profession. This anti-fiction lobby faced severe difficulties in attaining its ends because once libraries had begun to provide novels, and most did so right from the beginning, it was practically impossible to stop doing so without provoking harmful public reaction and inflicting serious damage on the service. Nevertheless, like many vocal pressure groups, it gained a high profile, and exerted some influence upon professional attitudes to fiction. The anti-fiction campaign had a number of facets: it was, in some instances, simply one against the provision of novels through the levied rates; in other instances, one against the payment by one group of people for the recreation of another group, and, in yet other cases, a reaction by librarians who, wishing to be seen to be public educators, felt that fiction provision contributed to a less than impressive professional image.

The agitation to stop libraries providing fiction originated in the profession itself. The basic arguments against fiction were straightforward and relatively unchanging, and were reiterated countless times at library conferences and in the professional press. The first major debate of the fiction question occurred as early as the second annual meeting of The Library Association in 1879, at which Taylor Kay, the librarian of Owens College in Manchester, presented a paper[1] in which he concluded that 'a hard and fast line must be drawn. A distinct refusal by library committees to purchase a single novel or tale would be appreciated by the ratepayers'. The basis of Kay's case against fiction was that the use of public money to provide amusement could not be justified, mainly because it involved middle-class ratepayers contributing to the recreational reading of working-class library users. It was also founded upon a concept of leisure as a luxury rather than as an integral element of social provision:

Now that school boards are fully established, and are succeeding so admirably in their great work, is it wise or necessary to place so much light literature in the hands of the people? – to find in these days of cheap literature and high wages, novels, presumably for the working man to read, free, or at the expense of ratepayers? The rates have already to be drawn upon towards educating his children, and some of his fellow-ratepayers may reasonably object to provide, in addition, the luxury of a novel, one of the cheapest luxuries purchasable. For novel-reading is a luxury, an amusement, a relaxation, and like all other luxuries should be paid for. Besides, the purchase of novels at the expense of ratepayers is an injustice to him, not an injustice to the ratepayer only, but to the recipient, for he is demoralized politically in being taught practically that he has a right to luxuries at the expense of his fellow-ratepayers.

Anticipating and dismissing the counter-argument that those who began by reading popular novels might eventually progress to better things, Kay went on to claim, correctly, that the demand for novels was not always unwelcome to librarians because it contributed so heavily to the impressive issue statistics that most public libraries could demonstrate. This was, however, a short-sighted approach, as the supply of fiction was detrimental not only to the image of the public library, but to the professional status of librarians: 'By the use to which a section of the public is putting the libraries, they are losing in dignity, in respect and in value . . . This enormous circulation of novels is degrading to a library, and especially to the librarian. His status will never rise whilst he is engaged in the circulation of novels'.

Kay also used the familiar argument that novel-reading incapacitated people for serious work and warped their judgment, and concluded by stating that a refusal to purchase fiction would enable libraries to attain their true educational character. Following the paper, there was a lively discussion of the motion, which was roundly defeated. Kay's arguments may seem typically Victorian in their preoccupation with funding recreation through the rates and with the expenditure of public money on 'ephemeral' literature. However, the argument that individuals should pay for their leisure has been a central issue in the debate of public sector leisure provision in recent years, as political ideology has nurtured a critical analysis of public sector leisure provision and promoted the introduction of private sector principles in local authority leisure. The fiction question was again discussed at the Library Association conference of 1883, when the predominant use of libraries by working-class readers was again a factor. In his opening address[2] Sir James Picton said that although the object of supplying a 'healthy source of recreation and amusement' to working-class users was praiseworthy, it had detracted from educational objectives.

The internal professional debate of fiction provision rumbled on for decades, reaching a climax in 1908 at roughly the same time that the Great Fiction Question gained its widest general notoriety. In a controversial paper[3] delivered to the Library Association's annual meeting, Mr A. Jennings, the chairman of the Brighton library committee, proposed that there was no justification for a public library spending ratepayers' money on books which were published simply for recreational reading and had no educational or literary value. He advocated a strict national policy in book selection to ensure that ephemeral novels read simply for leisure purposes would not be bought. His proposal is worth quoting in its entirety:

1. That the function of a public lending library is to provide good literature for circulation among its readers, and that the same test must be applied to its works of fiction, as to the books in its other departments, – they must have literary or educational value.

2. That every public lending library should be amply supplied with fiction that has attained the position of classical literature, such as the works of Scott, Dickens, Thackeray, George Eliot; and among the more modern writers Stevenson, Kipling, Meredith, Hardy. These names are, of course, merely given by way of illustration, and each library must be allowed to make its own rules as to the admission into the charmed circle, provided that it can satisfy its conscience that the suggested test has been applied.

3. That the purchase of mere ephemeral fiction of no literary, moral, or educational value, even if without offence, is not within the province of a public lending library.

A lengthy and acrimonious debate ensued, in which librarians and library committee men debated the proposal. Again, this was interesting not only for its insights to opinions on the merits of fiction, but for the extent to which they reflected attitudes to publicly-funded leisure. In contrast to the 'no amusement on the rates' faction, a number of contributors argued that amusement and recreation were *not* luxuries, but an essential element of modern civilized society, and that fiction was a valid means of providing these. Despite the fact that the motion was not binding and therefore had little practical significance, the debate of the topic and the almost unanimous support for the proposal were widely welcomed throughout the library profession.

MORE GENERAL CRITICISMS OF FICTION PROVISION

The feeling that the provision of fiction undermined the educational work of libraries was widely held outside the profession. In 1900, the *Daily News* complained that public libraries were 'storehouses of fiction' and encouraged recreative reading at the expense of educational objectives.[4] Criticisms of this nature stung, and provoked a defensive reaction from librarians and committee men; at Accrington, where the proposed adoption of the Libraries Acts in 1887 had been defeated through opposition to the likelihood of the library rate being used to purchase fiction, the chairman of the committee declared publicly, when the library was finally opened in 1901, that the committee was anxious that 'the proper class of books should be selected', as they did not wish the library to have a fiction issue of 95%.[5] Similar avowals that the demand for fiction would not deflect libraries from their educational priorities were made at the opening of Hornsey library in 1899.[6] Surprisingly, this sentiment was echoed by the popular novelist, Hall Caine, who thought that public libraries were too concerned with recreational as opposed to educational reading.[7]

Towards the close of the nineteenth century, the proportion of fiction and the extent of its borrowing became the subject of political discussion and were cited as an example of profligate municipal socialism. In 1891, a devastating attack, not only upon fiction provision but upon public libraries, was published by M.D. O'Brien in an edited collection *A plea for liberty: an argument against socialism and socialistic legislation.*[8] The main thrust of the attack was that: 'A Free Library may be defined as the socialist's continuation school. While State education is manufacturing readers for books, State-supported libraries are providing books for readers . . . A portion of our population has by legislation acquired the right to supply itself with necessaries and luxuries at the cost of the rates'. O'Brien ignored any serious consideration of the educational benefits of public libraries, declaring that he valued education rather lowly, believing that the only useful education for 95% of the population was a 'quick ear, a sharp eye, and a strong well-knit muscular frame', which was not to be obtained through schooling or formal education:

> . . . to listen to the advocates of Free Libraries one would imagine that these institutions were only frequented by students, and that the books borrowed were for the most part of a profound and scholarly character. But the very reverse of this is the case. The committee of the Blackpool Free Library, in their Report for the year 1887–8 say:- Works of fiction and light literature enjoy the greatest degree of popularity, each book circulating eleven times in the year, while the more instructive books in the other classes circulate only once during the same period.

Manipulating data from annual reports of several libraries, he demonstrated that similar proportions of fiction and non-fiction were borrowed elsewhere, and was thus able to argue that public libraries served the leisure interests of a minority through municipal rates:

> The truth is that a Free library favours one special section of the community
> – the book-readers – at the expense of all the rest. The injustice of such an
> institution is conspicuously apparent when it is remembered that
> temperaments and tastes are as varied as faces. If one man may have his
> hobby paid for by his neighbours, why not all? Are theatre-goers, lovers of
> cricket, bicyclists, amateurs of music, and others to have their earnings
> confiscated, and their capacities for indulging in their own special hobbies
> curtailed, merely to satisfy gluttons of gratuitous novel-reading?

O'Brien maintained that to provide any books, not just novels, to working-
class readers was to render them a disservice, as it did not encourage self-
reliance, and that conversely, there was no justification for 'poor women and
others, who are often the sole support of a large family of children', having
their hard-gained earnings taken from them to maintain well-to-do readers in
gratuitous literature. O'Brien's views were somewhat extreme, but they
reflected a widely held view that to supply fiction 'on the rates' was a
misappropriation of public money.

A similar politically motivated attack upon public library fiction appeared
four years later in a *New review* article 'The free library failure',[9] which conceded that while not even the 'most reactionary Tory' would deny that
libraries had some redeeming features, the public library movement in general
had been a failure, the chief reason being a lack of judgment in the selection of
books, most markedly in the 'absurd preponderance of fiction'. Again, it was
argued that fiction was cheap enough to be affordable to all, and that if it was
conceded that fiction should be provided in public libraries, it was impossible
to argue that other forms of recreation should not be similarly provided.

The accusations that the provision of popular novels through public money
for what was in truth a minority of the general public was, then as now, a
challenging assertion for the public library's supporters to answer. Even
where the public library service flourished, as it did in Sheffield, the Lord
Mayor of the city openly declared that he did not expect to get his amusement
in the form of light literature any more than his amusement in the form of
sport paid for by the public.[10] The most robust response to this came from
Thomas Greenwood, who, like Slaney and Brotherton before him, pointed out
that reading fiction was at least socially harmless, and was a relatively
inexpensive means of providing people with something to do:

> The two cries 'More rates' and 'Fiction' are somewhat closely connected
> inasmuch as it is generally sought to be shown that, for the additional
> payment, too much of an undesirable article is circulated. What a pity it is
> these strenuous advocates of municipal economy will not direct attention

to the much more serious questions of increases in poor and police rates, neither of which yield much return . . .

The actual amount of visible good which is accomplished by any ordinary municipal Library, when compared with the workhouse or the jail, bearing in mind the disproportionate expenditure, is so manifest that it is hard to believe that there are persons endowed with so much perversity as to miss observing it for themselves. Yet so it is, and as with the Fiction bogey so the Rate bogey is always being dragged forth to frighten ignorant ratepayers.[11]

The politically motivated anti-fiction views described in the above paragraphs have been a durable strand in right-wing theory, and recently formed the basis of the Adam Smith Institute's *Ex libris*.[12] The passage below, taken from this document, bears a striking resemblance to the anti-fiction arguments of a century ago:

In reality, a substantial part of the public library system is now devoted to the supply of free fiction and other light reading, much of it of little or no literary merit, to people who could afford to buy books but choose not to do so . . . attempts to elevate the status of the public library service from the mere lending of books to the vital application of information technology in the interests of greater economic growth are, in most parts of Britain, something of a nonsense. While the ambitious librarian may like to look on him or herself as part of a vital information industry, the bulk of library customers use the service as a publicly funded provider of free romantic fiction.

In the most forthright political critique of public libraries of the post-war decades, this report claimed that they had forced the closure of the commercial subscription libraries such as those operated by Boots and W. H. Smith, which thrived mainly upon fiction provision, through being able to offer a free service. It also noted that the expenditure of public money through libraries supported 'middle of the road' hardback novels that were not published in paperback, and that authors were compensated by the taxpayer through Public Lending Right rather than by borrowers. The proposed remedy was to end the tradition of free provision of novels and to introduce charges: '. . . the argument for making a charge for the borrowing of books is difficult to resist. There seems no good reason why the state should be expected to provide leisure and entertainment facilities of one kind free of charge to the user when it does not do so for others such as films or football'.

Like O'Brien's attack, *Ex libris* was in essence an attack upon the concept of public sector provision in general, but, unlike its predecessor, it reflected the dominant political ideology of the time and was the precursor of a green paper proposing the introduction of charges for certain elements of the public library service, including the borrowing of newly published fiction.[13] The main thrust of this proposal concerned the establishment of subscription schemes in lending departments under which newly published fiction would be available only to members paying a fee to obtain a premium level of service. Although this was proclaimed to be a revolutionary approach, it was in fact a revival of Victorian public library practice.

SUBSCRIPTION DEPARTMENTS IN PUBLIC LIBRARIES

In the nineteenth century, a number of towns, among them Warrington, Bolton, Stockport and Rochdale, established subscription schemes within their municipal public libraries. Their purpose was to raise funds to finance other aspects of the library service. Although the operation of these subscription libraries differed in minor detail from town to town, the normal practice was to run them alongside a free lending library. Readers able and prepared to pay a fee were allowed to borrow new books from the subscription library before these were transferred to the lending department, usually after one year, after which they could be borrowed by the general public under normal public library conditions. By this method, a library could generate funds, reduce or maintain the library rate, and provide a constant stream of one-year-old books into its lending stock.

In order to maximize their profitability, subscription libraries in public libraries had to have a popular appeal, and thus provided the books that subscribers would be prepared to pay for, which were, in the main, novels and other recreational books. At Rochdale, this resulted in 90% of the books in the subscription library being fiction or of a miscellaneous nature, and no books at all of science, politics or commerce.[14] At the close of its sixth year the Bolton subscription library was able to transfer 236 volumes to the free lending library,[15] this figure increasing to 1,133 volumes at the close of the thirtieth year. Indeed, by 1883, the issue from Bolton's subscription department was larger than that from the free lending department, and consisted almost entirely of recreational reading, its issue of 57,963 included 30,721 novels and 19,923 magazines.[16]

Such subscription libraries were patronized predominantly by middle-class borrowers and, at Bolton, where the subscribers included 139 women of 'superior position',[17] it was alleged that fee-paying subscribers placed working-class readers at a disadvantage by taking up a disproportionate amount of staff time.[18] John Potter Briscoe, a librarian who had at one time worked in Bolton library, concluded that the extra staff time involved in operating a subscription department was so great – the subscribers not unnaturally feeling that they had a greater claim upon the services of the library staff than the general public – that it seriously detracted from the financial benefits to be gained.[19] There is a strong likelihood that similar expectations of a premium level of customer service would be expressed today were the system to be reintroduced.

The sense of exclusion from the best available level of service in what was, after all, a public library, naturally provoked discontent among working-class readers. This occurred forcibly in Warrington, where the subscription library became the focus of a class conflict. Warrington was one of the first public libraries to be opened, and had its origins in an existing subscription library which was taken over by the town council. The subscription fee in 1850 was one guinea per annum,[20] which, although it was reduced to five shillings per annum in 1886, was still, as a contemporary observer remarked, 'just high enough to keep out the vulgar herd, though easily covered by the better-off'.[21] As was normally the case elsewhere, the Warrington subscription library was used primarily for obtaining fiction; in 1876, novels accounted for 83.6% of the 26,527 issues.[22] The exclusion from the subscription library of anyone who could not afford the fees, which, in effect, meant most working-class readers, became the topic of a long-running debate in the town and a lengthy campaign by a committee composed chiefly of working-class representatives finally succeeded in persuading the Conservative-dominated library committee to close the subscription library in 1891.

Subscription departments were sometimes vital in generating income to maintain the viability of a public library service. Wigan public library was opened in 1878, mainly as a result of two local benefactors, Thomas Taylor and Joseph Winnard, who donated considerable sums of money towards the erection of the library building and the purchase of a stock of books. A subscription scheme was considered at the time of the library's opening, but was rejected because most of those who expressed a willingness to join were already ratepayers and the library committee felt it was unfair to expect borrowers to pay twice for the use of the service. The library rate, however, proved to be inadequate to the development of the library, and before the library was barely five years old the librarian alerted the committee to the fact that many books were worn out through constant use, and that a shortage of funds was making it impossible to replace these.[23] The mediocre condition of the stock resulted in a sharp decrease in the issues of books, thus making stock renewal a priority, and when the idea of a subscription department to generate income for the purpose of providing new stock was discussed for a second time, it received approval.

The fee at Wigan's subscription library was one guinea per annum, the stated objective being to place 200 new books in the free lending library, although the librarian's annual report for 1883 commented that this seemed a modest figure in comparison with the daily losses being incurred.[24] The subscription library produced the desired results and, in 1884, 200 volumes were duly transferred to the lending library and the lending department's issues rose by over 5,000 to 57,046. The subscription department continued to provide a steady flow of new books to the free lending library until 1889, when it was closed as a result of the town council being able to provide a better level of funding to the library. The subscription department at Wigan thus appears to have owed more to political pragmatism rather than ideological conviction.

The radical challenge of the anti-fiction lobby and the operation of subscription departments are both relevant to modern developments in public libraries, most obviously in the views of the Adam Smith Institute and in the current political and ideological debate of the provision of public sector leisure facilities and services. While it is unlikely that libraries will not provide recreational books and other media, the introduction of compulsory competitive tendering in other areas of local authority leisure provision suggests that leisure aspects of libraries may be seen as an extra option to be charged for at point of service, possibly in the form of subscription schemes similar to those of a century ago. The historical development of these subscription departments shows that they introduced a two-level service, in which those who could afford to pay received a better service, not only through the inherent structure of the system which gave preferential access to new books, but through the fact that subscribers received a higher level of customer care from library staff.

The criticisms of libraries for providing leisure on the rates introduced economic and financial factors into what, until then, had been a discussion concerned primarily with social and moral benefits. The fact that the contribution of leisure to the life of a community is difficult to measure in quantifiable terms presents difficulties to public sector leisure managers, including librarians, and has led to a practice of evaluation based on easily measurable criteria such as participation rates and unit costs. This has several disadvantages, however, for the identification and attainment of social goals is difficult in competitive tendering and contracts based upon raw statistical performance indicators.[25]

Despite the forcefulness of its protagonists, the anti-fiction campaign achieved little real success, although it doubtlessly served to temper fiction provision in libraries where it found support among committee members. The fact that it existed at all demonstrates clearly that, even half a century after libraries were introduced, there was still fundamental confusion and disagreement, both within and outside the profession, about what public libraries were for.

NOTES AND REFERENCES TO CHAPTER 5

1 Kay, J. T., The provision of novels in rate-supported libraries, in *Transactions and proceedings of the 2nd annual meeting of The Library Association of the United Kingdom, Manchester, 1879*, 42–6.

2 *Transactions and proceedings of The Library Association of the United Kingdom, sixth annual meeting 1883*.

3 *Library Association record*, 1908, 534–41.

4 *Daily News*, 15 December 1900.

5 *Accrington Observer*, 30 March 1901.

6 *Library Association record*, 1, 1899, 789–91.

7 *Northern Daily Telegraph*, 3 November 1906.

8 O'Brien, M. D., 'Free libraries', in Mackay, T. (ed.), *A plea for liberty: an argument against socialism and socialistic legislation*, Murray, 1891, 329–49.

9 Roberts, W., 'The free library failure', *New review*, 13, 1895, 316–24.

10 *Sheffield Daily Telegraph*, 22 September 1909.

11 Greenwood, T., 'The great fiction question', *Libraries, Museums and Art Galleries yearbook*, Cassell, 1897, 107–16.

12 *Ex libris*, Adam Smith Institute, 1986.

13 *Financing our public library service: four subjects for debate: a consultative paper*, HMSO, 1988, Cm. 324.

14 Briscoe, J. P., 'Subscription libraries in connexion with free public libraries', in *Transactions and proceedings of the first annual meeting of The Library Association of the United Kingdom held at Oxford 1878*, 19–23.

15 Bolton Public Library, *Sixth annual report*, 1859.

16 Bolton Public Library, *Thirtieth annual report*, 1883

17 Great Britain, House of Commons, *Further returns relating to the Free Libraries Acts* 1877. It was also observed at the Library Association's conference of 1893 that subscription libraries were used by professional men, mainly for fiction.

18 *Bolton Journal and Guardian*, 27 July 1906.

19 Briscoe, op. cit., ref. 14.

20 One guinea was 21 shillings, or £1.05 in decimal currency.

21 *Warrington Examiner*, 13 March 1886.

22 Warrington Public Library, *Annual report*, 1876

23 Wigan Public Library, *Annual Report*, 1882.

24 Wigan Public Library, *Annual Report*, 1883.

25 Stabler, M. and Ravenscroft, N., 'The economic evaluation of output in public leisure services', *Leisure studies*, 13 (2), April 1994, 111–33.

Chapter 6

Fiction and the Popularization of Libraries

Positive approaches to fiction

In contrast to the anti-fiction camp, there were many librarians and committee members who actively supported the provision of both literary and popular novels in public libraries. In some instances, this was for the pragmatic reason that only popular fiction could generate the desired high levels of use. In other cases, it was based on the more liberal notion that recreational reading was a valid leisure activity in its own right, a concept which represented an important development in public sector leisure provision. In several cases the motivating factor was a desire to promote rational recreation, and in this sense public libraries fulfilled the hopes of many of their protagonists. In other towns, fiction was just one element in a wide-ranging provision of leisure within an urban paternalist framework. The evidence provided by library catalogues and statistics of issues suggests that, whatever the rhetoric on fiction at conferences and in the press, a relatively open approach to fiction was adopted in many authorities. The rationales for such approaches were a complex mixture of the factors outlined immediately above.

Although the evidence of the 1849 Select Committee shows that the provision of fiction as a form of rational recreation was anticipated before libraries were introduced, it was not as frequently found as an explicit rationale after the 1850 Act. Nevertheless, the Liverpool library committee openly expressed its pleasure that fiction issues were providing a socially beneficial pastime for borrowers, commenting in its first annual report in 1852 that 'Works of amusement form about one half of all the books read. Far from regretting this result, the committee feel it their duty to render this portion of the library more attractive still, being of the opinion that love of reading in any form must tend to counteract the propensity to low and degrading pursuits'.[1] Indeed, Peter Cowell, the librarian at Liverpool, claimed to know personally of some cases in which reading novels had prevented 'indulgence in a much worse pursuit'.[2] Most libraries, however, provided fiction simply because there was a demand for it, and because it attracted the public. Many librarians resented this fact, but, as Bramwell, the librarian at Preston, pointed out, those libraries which made a stand against fiction were those which had the fewest visitors.[3]

Although it was necessary to supply fiction to popularize libraries, it was sometimes felt that this was rather over-done. This produced the paradox identified by McAllister, the editor of *The library* in an article revealingly titled 'New ways of keeping down the issue of fiction',[4] that in practice public libraries encouraged and promoted excessive issues of fiction, while librarians simultaneously deplored this very excess. The ideal many librarians hoped for was to obtain an overall rise in the number of books issued, while achieving a decrease or, at worst, a relatively small increase in the issue of novels. George Elliott, the librarian at Belfast, proudly pointed out that the 61.2% of the issue represented by fiction in his library compared favourably with Birmingham's 64.2%, Manchester's 78.4% and Liverpool's 79.9%.[5] Such achievements were relatively rare, however, and the pressure to maintain or increase issues in order to demonstrate an acceptable level of use continued, prompting the accusation that libraries bought the 'veriest twaddle' written, to swell the issue figures.[6]

Much ingenuity was invested in manipulating issue statistics to disguise the high proportions of high fiction borrowing. Sunderland public library categorized literary novelists such as Austen, Dickens, Eliot and Scott as classical English literature in its issues; this did not reduce the overall issue of fiction, but it did minimize the percentage occupied by popular fiction, while at the same time it demonstrated that not all fiction borrowing was focused on popular novels.[7] The most sophisticated effort of this kind came from Thomas Greenwood, who demonstrated that, taken in the context of the whole output of public libraries, fiction lending represented only 25% of the total issues, and that in lending departments, where the average fiction issue was 60–65%, fiction represented only 30% of the total lending stock.[8]

A frequently encountered argument in support of fiction was that reading popular novels was the first step to reading literary fiction or, better still, works of criticism and philosophy. This was neatly expressed in a description of a day's reading in Glasgow's Mitchell Library where, it was reported, a reader might progress from basic beginnings to higher works as part of a 'refining process' in which the 'whole tone of a man's being, moral and intellectual', was raised through his immersion in literary culture.[9] This was suggested as early as 1869 by Edward Edwards,[10] and, almost 30 years later, Taylor, the librarian at Brentford, published a defence of fiction reading[11] based upon such an actuality, a reader having begun with Captain Marryat,

Mayne Reid and Henty, progressed to Scott, and gradually to non-fiction and the history of the period of Scott's novels. Such cases were, however, the exception rather than the rule; certainly, Peter Cowell found little evidence in Liverpool to support this theory.[12]

From the 1880s onwards, there was an emerging acceptance that public library fiction did not have to be justified solely on the utilitarian grounds of self-improvement or social order. The recognition of the validity of recreational reading for its own sake took some time to develop, but by the early twentieth century, Manchester public library had elevated it into a principle of policy, the librarian, Credland, claiming that

> 'we are bound to supply books of healthy recreation in the form of light literature . . . if we stock one kind of book to interest and entertain one class, we can be legitimately called upon to stock another kind of book for another class. The class of lowly education has quite as good a claim to consideration as have their more highly educated brothers.[13]

A similarly liberal approach to fiction provision also existed outside the profession. Canon Barry, speaking in support of the Worcester public library, declared that there was nothing he enjoyed better than a good light book;[14] another clergyman said, at the opening of Bolton's library in 1893, that light reading was a legitimate leisure activity for tired workpeople.[15]

At its most robust, this form of fiction advocacy refused to adopt any tone of apology for its provision in public libraries, and argued instead that non-purposeful recreational reading was a legitimate and acceptable pastime, a view which has been widely held, though not unanimously, in British librarianship throughout most of the twentieth century. Not only librarians claimed this for fiction, for it was a view shared by some library committee members, such as Alderman Johnson, Chairman of Birmingham's library committee, who described fiction as not merely an amusement but, for working people, a 'necessary counterpoise to the monotony of mere mechanical employment'.[16] Similar attitudes were sometimes found in the local and national press, a *Northern Daily Telegraph* editorial in 1906 commenting approvingly on the reading of library novels as a form of relaxation and diversion.[17] Even Greenwood felt compelled to concede that arcane works were of little value to exhausted labourers and that it was unreasonable to criticize working-class people for their enjoyment of undemanding popular novels.[18]

As with many aspects of the library service, the practice of providing ample stocks of popular fiction depended largely upon local factors, most notably the intentions of the library committee. Indeed, to understand fully how the public library service developed it is essential to appreciate that it was very much a locally provided service which reflected the beliefs and vision of its governing body. This element is missed in generalized overviews of library development, and to provide a deeper insight to how and why libraries reacted in differing ways to the provision of fiction, the remainder of this chapter and the following chapter use case studies based upon the library services of Blackburn, Wigan and Darwen – three northern industrial towns which adopted the Libraries Acts at a relatively early date and which were therefore confronted with the fiction problem as it arose. These three towns shared a number of common characteristics, having grown rapidly as a result of industrialization and having many of the social problems associated with this. They show how a demand for fiction was quickly expressed, and how local political, economic and social factors had an influence upon the way in which the library responded to this.

FICTION AND THE POPULAR LIBRARY: BLACKBURN

Blackburn is the principal town in north-east Lancashire. Although it has suffered enormous economic decline in recent decades, it was, in the period between 1850 and the First World War, a prosperous borough with a range of textile and engineering industries based on cotton, with over 37,000 employees working in 130 cotton mills in 1902. When it opened its library in 1862, it was the twenty-third town to adopt the Public Libraries Acts.

Despite having provided a library from a relatively early date, Blackburn was never considered to be a progressive library authority. It was, for example, frequently criticized for its outdated methods of lending books, and initially the systems for obtaining books were somewhat inefficient, as borrowers could select either from a printed catalogue or from a shelf of recently returned books, most of which were novels. As a correspondent to the *Blackburn Times* noted in 1894, a member could either 'poke about' among the returned books on the library counter, which were not arranged in any order, or could ask the library assistant for a book.[19] If the requested book were on loan to another reader, which, according to the writer of the letter was not an unusual occurrence, the assistant would usually offer another book by the same author.

The time allowed for reading a novel and the rate of fines on overdue books were also publicly criticized. The loan period was two weeks for non-fiction but only one week for fiction, with fines charged at six pence per week in 1901. This compared unfavourably with conditions in other local libraries; nearby Darwen, for example, allowed 14 days for novels and had a fine-rate of one penny per week.

The book selection process was regulated by the library committee, which delegated responsibility for the selection of books to a sub-committee.

Librarians had little say in what was purchased, but were simply left to implement the mechanics of ordering chosen titles. Immediately before the opening, the librarian, William Abram, was instructed to visit booksellers to purchase the titles chosen by the book selection sub-committee, and this mode of practice continued for many decades. This formal approach to book selection was rigidly maintained: the library committee minutes of 1877 suggest that the librarian may have lapsed into making unauthorized purchases: '. . . on all occasions prior to making a purchase of a book, or books, for the Library . . . [the Librarian] shall consult the Chairman on the subject, and if considered necessary, a meeting of the Book Selection Sub-Committee shall be called as the case may require'.[20] It is worth noting the extent of the chairman's power, who alone could make decisions on book purchases without necessarily referring to anyone else.

Nevertheless, despite these relatively antiquated and severe conditions, Blackburn library developed a tradition of providing what its reading public wanted, which was, predominantly, popular fiction. Novels and light reading materials were plentifully stocked from the beginning, and of the 90 pages of the first catalogue, over 12 were devoted to prose fiction, and featured Dickens, Bulwer Lytton, Fielding, Mrs Gaskell, Scott, Thackeray, the Brontës and other standard novelists whose works were normally purchased by public libraries as a matter of course. It is impossible to determine precisely the number of novels issued in the library's early years because, like many other public library authorities, Blackburn used a very broad classification system, fiction being subsumed in Literature and Polygraphy, which also included poetry and essays. The lending department's issues in the first two years show that Literature and Polygraphy, which included fiction, constituted roughly 60% of the total issue. The report for 1862–3[21] was more revealing, citing some of the books in heaviest demand; they included Dickens' *Christmas books*, Fielding's *Amelia* and Ainsworth's *Mervyn Clitheroe*. A similar pattern prevailed in the following year, in which fiction accounted for two-thirds of the Literature and Polygraphy class, with the most popular novels being Collins' *The woman in white* (42 issues), Dickens' *Nicholas Nickleby* (50 issues), Ainsworth's *Ovingdean Grange* (43 issues) and Lever's *Martins of Cro' Martin* (42 issues).[22]

The large issues of fiction in this period were seen not as an embarrassment, as they often were in other towns, but as evidence of the library's utility. The annual report for 1863–4 calculated the average number of times a book from each class was issued and thus demonstrated the cost-effectiveness of purchasing popular novels (see Table 6.1).

Table 6.1 Comparative number of times books issued

Class	Number of volumes in stock	Average number of times each book issued
1. Theology and Philosophy	105	3
2. History	1,478	3.5
3 Politics and Commerce	108	1.75
4. Sciences and Art	360	4.25
5. Literature and Polygraphy	1,474	11.75

The demand for fiction grew in the 1870s,, and by the end of the decade fiction accounted for 85% of the lending department's issue. The extent of the demand for fiction in Blackburn becomes clearer when it is taken into account that this was a feature of the reference department too. The issue of standard reference works was far outstripped by the demand for novels; in 1865, Braddon's *Lady Audley's secret* was issued 53 times from the reference library, Collins' *Woman in white* 52 times and *The Pickwick papers* 49 times. The report for 1864–5[23] observed that the chief demand in both the lending and the reference departments was for light literature, and pointed out that most requests in the reference department were for novels and illustrated magazines rather than for scientific or technical publications. There was, in fact, some concern about the poor rate of use of the reference department, but the suggested remedy to this was not to encourage the reading of textbooks but to put more novels into the reference library to attract readers to it.

The gradual increases in the issue of fiction were noticed by the librarian and the committee, and from the late 1860s attracted comment in the annual reports. In 1867, the librarian observed that:

> Although the Library contains an excellent and extensive collection of some of the best Biographies, Histories, Travels and Essays, the demand for these does not realize the anticipations of some members of the Committee who are anxious to encourage the reading of instructive Histories and Travels; indeed it is most surprising that some of the most interesting and fascinating books of Modern Times are comparatively so little called for.[24]

Not only were the 'instructive' books little used, but the demand for fiction outstripped its·supply: 'Although the Committee have, during the year, considerably increased the number of volumes in the Class Literature and Polygraphy, which includes works of Fiction and Miscellaneous Literature, yet the demand by borrowers for books of this description is greatly in excess of the supply, four-fifths of the total issue being from this class'.[25] In his report for 1869, David Geddes, the librarian, presented a more explicit account of the demand for popular fiction:

> In popular literature the demand has been greatly in excess of the supply . . . the works of Dickens, Bulwer Lytton, Mayne Reid, Marryat, Lever, Scott, Disraeli, Cooper, Mrs. Henry Wood and other popular authors, are literally read to pieces, although there are more than one copy of some of the popular volumes in the library; in many instances repeated application has to be made before a borrower can obtain the use of a volume of some favourite author.[26]

In particular, borrowers wanted sensation novels: 'Borrowers who read sensational literature are the most difficult to satisfy, as they are continually enquiring for the most recent and popular works of that description; indeed it would be vain to attempt to supply the demand in some instances, even were it advisable to do so'.[27]

By the 1870s the high issues of fiction were a perennial topic of remark in the library's annual reports. Geddes realized there was a relationship between the provision of fiction and the popularity of the library, and, instead of resisting the demand for fiction, urged the committee to provide more novels still:

> The ever increasing demand for additional works in the Lending Department also renders it necessary that constant additions should be made to it, as the demand for certain books is at present beyond the means of supply; all the works of some popular Authors are always in the hands of the borrowers, so that repeated application has to be made to obtain any one of such works.[28]

The response to the fiction question in Blackburn in the early 1870s was to satisfy it as far as was reasonably possible. The library committee's primary objective was to encourage and promote the use of the library, and what was read was of secondary importance to this. Nevertheless, Geddes regretted the fact that many borrowers joined the library simply to borrow novels and ceased to visit it when they had read as many of their desired novels as the library could offer.[29] The relentless demand for novels and the necessity of replacing worn-out fiction placed a continuous strain on the library's resources, yet no significant steps were taken to reduce the fiction issue or to persuade borrowers to read anything other than fiction.

Further purchases of popular fiction

In the early 1890s there was a marked rise in the issue of fiction as Blackburn library continued to respond positively to the demand for popular fiction by purchasing as many novels as practically possible. The adoption of this purchasing policy coincided with the period of office of William Abram as the chairman of the library committee. Abram presents an interesting figure as a library committee chairman in that he had been Blackburn's first librarian, and had resigned from this post in 1867 to become editor of the *Blackburn Times*, the principal local newspaper. He was elected to the town council in 1878, and although he left this in 1884, he remained a coopted member of the library committee until 1894, acting as its chairman between 1890 and this date. At the beginning of the 1890s, the library already possessed a good stock of works by popular novelists, with several multiple copies of works by James Grant (57 titles, 114 copies), Mary Braddon (49 titles, 81 copies) and Mrs Henry Wood (32 titles, 90 copies). These generous levels of provision notwithstanding, substantial additions of popular fiction were made to the lending department, and this exercised a dramatic effect on the issues. Later in the decade, when there was a reduction in the number of new novels added, there was a corresponding decrease in the issues. Table 6.2 illustrates the relationships between fiction purchase and borrowing figures. Literature and Polygraphy, the class which included fiction, had by this time been renamed as Class E.

Table 6.2   The impact of fiction purchases on the issues

Year ending	Books added to Class E	Total issue	Class E issue
1889	298	55,702	49,734
1890	1,225	61,817	55,879
1891	1,389	71,202	65,864
1892	1,306	88,189	79,886
1893	935	95,954	86,175
1894	591	102,025	91,674
1895	649	118,463	108,725
1896	592	86,628	74,034
1897	468	92,259	78,525
1898	497	82,981	70,378

As can be seen, there was a close correlation between the number of additions to Class E and the issues of books both from that class and from the total departmental issue. If the performance of the library was to be measured in terms of issues, as Geddes had earlier suggested, then an adequate provision of popular fiction was essential to success in these terms. The majority of the novels added in 1890 were by popular authors, among them the complete works of Emma Worboise, Rita, Florence Marryat, Wilkie Collins, James Payn, Mayne Reid, Farjeon and Harrison Ainsworth.[30] The decision to satisfy what was evidently a huge demand for popular fiction was based upon the objective of demonstrating the usefulness of the library by making it a popular public institution. New books were bought in proportion to the demand, multiple copies of the most popular novels were provided, and an extensive rebinding policy ensured that well-thumbed novels were not out of circulation longer than was necessary. In the library's annual report for 1891–2, Richard Ashton, then the librarian, explained this equation of popularity with utility: 'By the action of the Committee in the continuous purchase of what is called current literature, new works, and new editions as fast as they are announced, with extra copies of those in demand, and by the speedy and substantial manner in which books worn with much use are rebound, the usefulness of the library is fully maintained'.[31]

An interview with Richard Ashton in the *Preston Herald* in 1890[32] offered a deeper insight to the nature of the demand for fiction. There was, he said, little demand in Blackburn for any books other than those of fiction, travel or history. The most popular novelists were Rider Haggard, David C. Murray, Robert Louis Stevenson, Marion Crawford, Grant Allen and Hall Caine. Fiction by female novelists was also in demand, the most popular writer being Edna Lyall:

> . . . it is very seldom that her *Donovan, We two, In the golden days* and *Knight Errant* can be procured at first demand. Mrs. Henry Wood has, of course, many followers, but for some little time her popularity has been gradually diminishing. Amongst the other lady writers who have acquired great notoriety may be mentioned Mrs. Young, George Eliot, Miss Braddon, Miss Austen, Miss Worboise and the sisters Brontë.

Ashton admitted that a similar pattern of demand for fiction prevailed in the reference library, where fiction and miscellaneous literature accounted for 60% of that department's issue.

Much as the library's fiction selection policies must have been welcomed by borrowers, they provoked discontent in certain quarters. Some of this disillusion was based on a perception that, like the town's Mechanics' Institute, the public library's initial educational objectives had been undermined and eventually overwhelmed by the demand for recreation. A correspondent to the *Blackburn Standard*[33] questioned the extent to which the library was fulfilling its educational functions in providing so much popular fiction:

> A great majority of the people who make use of the library seem to think that its sole use is to supply them with light literature – i.e. novels and romances &c at a very cheap rate. One is delighted to see the stream of people passing in and out of our Free Library, but it is disappointing to know that a large percentage of them ask for and obtain books of the E class ... As a consequence of this a large and increasing stock of this type of book is kept; new novels and new editions of old novels have constantly to be bought to meet the demand.

A further critical letter was published in the same paper the following week,[34] this time anonymously, by a writer claiming to have been a member of the first library committee, who agreed with this criticism and claimed that it was never intended that the library, which had originally been established to provide instructive books for working men, should have become an institution for the supply of books which were not only of no practical utility, but which 'on the contrary, promote the habit of, and the craving for, sensational or even if simply amusing, still altogether uninstructive works of fiction'.

Reducing the fiction issue

In 1894, Samuel Crossley became chairman of the library committee, and a radical change in the approach to fiction provision ensued. Like Abram, Crossley took a keen and active interest in the affairs of the library, although his leadership style was more autocratic. A minor though revealing facet of this was that he himself wrote and signed the library's annual reports, a privilege normally accorded to the librarian both at Blackburn and elsewhere. Crossley's reports differed from those produced earlier in their greater emphasis on and discussion of the library's educational objectives, and in their gradual tendency to devote more space to the museum and art gallery. Crossley intended to curb the demand for and supply of fiction and to encourage a greater educational use of the library, but the durability of fiction's popularity proved resistant to his efforts.

His first task as chairman was to redefine the terms of reference of the book selection sub-committee and to issue a reminder that, in terms of book purchase, this committee had exclusive and absolute power. The immediate effect of this was a little-publicized decision to reduce drastically the purchase of new fiction titles. The outcome of this policy was the largest recorded reduction in the issue of the lending department since the opening of the library, a fall of 32,000, or 26%. Serious though this decline in the popularity of the library was, Crossley was apparently unmoved by it; it was simply irrelevant in terms of the newly-emphasized educational priorities of the library, to which the issue of novels contributed little. Indeed, in the few instances that this decrease in the issues was acknowledged, it was done so in a somewhat cavalier fashion: it was, as Crossley wrote, only the readers of novels who had neglected to renew their library memberships.[35] The former policy of providing novels in response to demand was abandoned in favour of the promotion of educational and instructive reading, and, in the annual report for 1902,[36] Crossley outlined the library's redefined objective: 'The Committee feel that the primary object of a Library maintained out of public funds is the provision and distribution of works likely to instruct and cultivate the minds of the readers rather than of novels for the mere diversion of readers'. It is difficult to tell whether this was a change of direction by the committee or simply a case of Crossley using the committee as a cover for his personal intentions. Whatever the case may have been, the result of this policy was an increased budget for the reference library and for 'books other than novels' for the lending library. However, the most interesting feature of this volte-face is that, despite Crossley's protestations and intentions, the library's major purchases continued to be of fiction and miscellaneous literature. Although fewer novels were bought than in previous years, in relative terms more fiction continued to be bought than of any other category of book. The massive reduction in the purchases of fiction and the related decrease in the library's popularity would inevitably have resulted in some public expression of discontent had this state of affairs continued. However, a sub-committee was established to investigate the massive reduction in the issue and to recommend ways of reversing the library's decline in popularity; its advice was that delivery stations should be established in the town's residential areas, the main function of which, although it was not openly declared, would be to revitalize the popularity of the library by providing ready access to fiction for the town's working-class population.

Delivery stations

Delivery stations were, in essence, a simple form of branch library, being service points that held no stock but which were housed in shops in which the owner would act as an agent for the library by taking requests for books, ordering them from the central library, and issuing them to borrowers on behalf of the library. The issue from the first two delivery stations to be opened was overwhelmingly of fiction; by 1908, there were eight delivery stations of whose aggregate issues fiction represented 95%. Between 1907 and 1914, the aggregate issue of fiction from Blackburn's public libraries remained between 35,000 and 40,000 annually, and although the reports continued to comment approvingly on the decrease in the issue of novels from the central library, in reality all that had occurred was that the provision of fiction had been diverted to the delivery stations, leaving the central library statistics to give the misleading impression that the demand for fiction had been overcome. The work of the delivery stations received very little notice in the annual reports which continued, as usual, to dwell on the central library, museum and art gallery.

Gradually, the strictures on fiction purchase were relaxed, though any apparent increase in the issue of non-fiction continued to generate enthusiasm among members of the library committee. When quantitative evidence was in short supply, Crossley employed subjective impressions to reassure the ratepayers, and perhaps even himself, that the library was still an agent for improving reading, as in the following remark: 'There is a slight increase in the total issue of books, but, though the statistics do not show it, there has been marked improvement in the class of reading in the Reference Library'.[37] The most significant progress in reducing the issue of fiction was achieved in the reference department, again, largely due to the establishment of the delivery stations, but, overall, the total issue of fiction from Blackburn's public libraries remained consistently in the range of 75% to 80% of the aggregate issue until the outbreak of war in 1914.

The determining factors of fiction provision in Blackburn

The most notable features of the library service in Blackburn were that the major uses of the library were for leisure purposes, and that book selection remained under the strict control of the library committee. For much of the period until the mid-1890s, there was little concern for what was being read; instead, the borrowing of popular fiction was adopted as a measure of the library's utility. Few members of the library committee took an active role in improving popular reading through library lectures, book selection practices or cooperative work with other agencies, as occurred in some towns.

The treatment of fiction in Blackburn library was determined not primarily by the actions of the librarians nor by contemporary professional ideologies relating to fiction, for neither of these had much influence upon practice. The major factor was the library committee and the characteristics of the men serving upon it, and, with this in view, it is useful to evaluate the management of the library service in the overall context of the town council.

The outstanding feature of local government in Blackburn before the First World War was the dominance of the Conservative party and the alliance between the council and the Church of England. This Anglican-Tory elite exercised power not only in the council chambers but in many areas of civic life; the Mechanics' Institute, for example, was dominated by the Conservative party and the Church of England and was once criticized by

Abram for its refusal to allow non-conformists to serve on its board of management.[38] The influence of the Church of England in Blackburn was augmented through the fact that many of the town's economic elite – the leading manufacturers and merchants – were Anglicans, and even though there was a considerable non-conformist presence in the town, this failed to exert any real influence upon municipal affairs. This control was maintained partly through the electoral process, and partly through the promotion of Conservative councillors to the aldermanic benches. To convey the hegemonic nature of Conservative control, it is worth citing the composition of the council in two separate years: in 1902, 13 of the 14 aldermen were Conservatives, and there were 25 Conservative, 11 Liberal and 6 Independent or Labour councillors,[39] and in 1909 12 of the 13 aldermen were Conservative, with the Conservatives holding an overall council majority of 35.[40] It is in such a context of Conservative tradition that the actions of the library committee should be assessed.

Fiction provision and the paternalist tradition

The library committee functioned as a sub-committee of the Free Library, Museum and Art Gallery Committee of the town council. Notable features of this committee were its large size and its frequent use of coopted members, many of whom were called upon for their knowledge of scientific and naturalist subjects, which was required for the operation of the museum; in 1900, for instance, it comprised four elected members of the council and seven coopted members. Like the town council itself, the library committee was dominated by Conservatives, with just a small proportion of Liberal representation. Under this Conservative committee, the pattern of service until the mid-1890s, when Crossley became chairman of the library committee, was to provide popular novels in response to public demand. Even though some of the librarians expressed misgivings about the extent of the supply of popular fiction, they were virtually powerless to restrain the committee's wish to purchase enough fiction to satisfy demand, especially in Abram's period of office between 1890 and 1894.

This approach to fiction provision is more clearly understood if it is seen in the context of a tradition of paternalist relationships between Blackburn manufacturers and employees. The evolution of an urban paternalism and the maintenance of social harmony in northern industrial towns through the demonstration by factory owners of an active interest in the lives of their employees, are well established.[41, 42, 43] A recent study of paternalism in Blackburn[44] has shown how the existence of a strong tradition of political and religious deference to employers, who were in the main Conservatives, was largely responsible for the notable lack of success of other political parties.

This deference was partly founded upon a perception of a shared economic dependency on a competitive cotton industry, and was strengthened by the provision of a varied range of leisure opportunities. Works outings, mill football teams, factory reading rooms and libraries were typical forms of leisure encouraged and supported by factory owners as a demonstration of goodwill towards and unity with their work-force. This interventionist approach to working-class leisure was essentially self-interested, and reflected a concept of leisure in which recreation was structurally beneficial to the whole community. There was often considerable overlap in nineteenth-century industrial towns between economic, social and political leadership, and this was certainly so in Blackburn, where the town council was ruled by an economically powerful elite. The domination of the council by industrialists and professional men reproduced this paternalist culture in municipal leisure provision, under which the provision of popular fiction in the library, together with the relative lack of action to promote the reading of better literature, was accepted with few questions. In sanctioning the use of the library for the acquisition of recreative reading, the library committee and the council facilitated a relatively harmless form of recreation and, in doing so, provided a council-operated library service which demonstrably acted in accordance with the wishes of the great majority of its users. To have censored or suppressed fiction, as occurred in some towns, would have been to be seen to act against the interests of the people. Abram himself, in an article in the *Fortnightly review* in 1868,[45] wrote of the moral responsibility of mill owners to demonstrate some interest in the social conditions of their employees, and compared this with the duty of a municipal authority to care for the health and happiness of its citizens. A town council could, he said, achieve this through the provision of various forms of leisure facility, including public libraries:

> Outside the mill too, the operative is not uncared for. The lavish provision of public parks, pleasure grounds, baths and free libraries in all the larger Lancashire towns, testifies that the corporate authorities are not unmindful of their obligations to promote the health, happiness, and culture of the industrial orders.
>
> The effect of these changes upon both the moral and physical condition of the operatives is most apparent. Far seldomer than of yore do we hear the murmur of popular discontent.

The appointment to the chairmanship of the library committee of Samuel Crossley, who was a solicitor and not an industrial employer, introduced a change of emphasis in the library's policy. However, this resulted in only a short-term change in fiction provision, as the decreased use of the library forced the library committee to investigate and establish delivery stations, thus facilitating once again the borrowing of popular novels.

In Blackburn, there was a positive and relatively open-minded approach to fiction throughout most of the pre- First World War era. Other public libraries, however, had greater ambitions, in terms of educational and reference work, than Blackburn, and fiction and other leisure aspects of the service were neglected. In the short term, such neglect was not serious, but if allowed to develop over a number of years, the emphasis on education and information at the expense of leisure could endanger the viability of the service. The development of Wigan public library provides an example of a service which began by concentrating almost exclusively upon reference and information services, but which was finally forced to acknowledge that the provision of fiction and recreational literature was essential to a public library's viability.

FICTION AND THE SCHOLARLY LIBRARY: WIGAN

Wigan adopted the Public Libraries Acts in 1876, when two local benefactors donated funds to erect a library building and to stock this with books, with the intention that Wigan should develop a reference library to compare with the scholarly libraries of the universities. The library's greatest ally in pursuit of this goal was the chairman of its library committee, James Ludovic Lindsay, the twenty-sixth Earl of Crawford and the ninth Earl of Balcarres. Lindsay was a noted bibliophile and his private library at Haigh Hall housed a collection of books, manuscripts and maps of international standing. He was a coopted member of the Wigan library committee from its opening until his death in 1913, and was President of The Library Association in 1898. He valued learning, scholarship and bibliographical excellence highly, and these became the hallmarks of Wigan's public library; indeed, the progress, or lack of it, of the lending department can only be fully appreciated in the context of the obsession with the reference department. The scholarly aspirations of the library were reflected in the design of the reference department, which imitated that of an old college library, having a central aisle flanked by ceiling-height bookcases and a first-floor gallery which can still be seen today. Unlike many library committees, which appointed men with no real qualification to act as librarians, Wigan's library committee took care to find someone with the ability to establish and develop a scholarly style of reference service and, in 1877, appointed Henry Tennyson Folkard, who had previously worked at the Royal Academy. Folkard served as Wigan's librarian until his death in 1916, and thus had an unbroken association of almost 40 years with the library, during which he was able to develop a service which reflected his knowledge and bibliographical expertise. Most unusually, he was entrusted with some responsibility for book selection, and was encouraged to acquire rare books or manuscripts for the reference library as they became available. Through Folkard's acquisitions of the best reference texts and Lindsay's regular donations of works from his private library, Wigan's reference department became nationally famous for its learned stock, which included several books and manuscripts not normally found in a public library. Unlike Blackburn's reference department, there was no popular fiction; Dickens, Smollett, Hugo, Diderot and Zola were to be found there, but not Braddon, Wood, Grant or Ouida.

Fiction in Wigan library

Wigan's lending department was always of secondary importance to the reference department. It was situated on the ground floor of the library, and proved, almost from the outset, to be too small in both floor area and shelf capacity. The members of the lending library were in the main drawn from the working class, and comprised a substantial proportion of women (see Table 6.3).

Table 6.3 Occupational groups of readers registered in Wigan lending library 1879

Clerks and bookkeepers	519
Wives and daughters	409
Colliers	201
Schoolmasters	170
Moulders and fitters	116
Factory operatives	116

Most of the borrowers were under 30 years of age.

Consistent with the scholarly library service Wigan wished to develop, the lending department contained many books on Science and Art, but the biggest single category was Fiction and Juvenile. The merging of these two categories tends to obscure, perhaps intentionally, the true proportion of fiction provision, for this category comprised over half of the library's stock by 1899. Despite the emphasis upon reference work, the library was mainly used for obtaining fiction. Between 1877 and 1914, the lending issue of fiction and juvenile literature was never less than 63% of the total, and in 25 of these years, it was greater than 80%.

The lack of adequate funding throughout the library's early years and the resulting reduction in the purchase of new books caused a drop in the issues and the ensuing establishment of the subscription library, which was discussed in Chapter 5. Unlike Blackburn, there was little inclination to interpret the demand for fiction in a positive light, although Folkard was sufficiently realistic to acknowledge that the lending department would always be more popular than the reference department in quantitative terms, as his comment in the annual report for 1889 shows:[46]

> The comparative usefulness of the several departments of the Institution will always be a matter for argument, but the figures set forth in this Report are probably sufficient to show that during the last ten years every department has worked well and grown in public favour. Necessarily in the lending branch Fiction will always be the greatest attraction. The figures for 1888 show this remarkably, for, out of a total issue of 68,430 volumes, no fewer than 56,897 were novels, the next highest section – poetry, drama and miscellaneous literature – only reaching 4,765 while science and art claimed 3,406. The actual proportion of novels to the whole collection in the lending Library is 4,631 to 5,507, so that relatively speaking, the supply of the recreative element, as compared with the educational, is decidedly in favour of the former. But the steady growth of attendances upstairs [i.e. the reference library] shows that for educational purposes the Institution is steadily accomplishing its object, especially among students in mining and mechanics, elementary educational teachers, and other people, to whom the books of reference are a veritable mine of wealth.

Some idea of the extent of fiction provision in Wigan's lending department can be gleaned from the departmental catalogue of 1903, which shows that there was a reasonable supply of titles by popular writers (see Table 6.4).

Table 6.4 Works by popular novelists in Wigan lending department in 1903

Author	Titles in stock	Copies in stock
Mary Braddon	60	115
Rhoda Broughton	13	15
Marie Corelli	15	20
James Grant	52	56
Ouida	24	29
Mrs. H. Wood	29	98

Neither the librarian nor the committee expressed much interest in the lending library or in what was being borrowed, and on the few occasions that it was mentioned in annual reports, it was with reference to its cramped conditions. There was no active campaign against fiction; it was simply not an important aspect of the service in comparison with the reference library. Even though the emphasis was upon reference services, the committee recognized the necessity of providing recreational services to ensure a viable degree of use of the library, as the following comment by a councillor shows: 'books of light literature in the shape of novels ought to be provided for those who visited the Library. If their Library was to maintain its present popularity, it seemed to him they would have to cater for the recreative as well as the educational wants of their readers',[47] and there were frequent stock additions of fiction, usually in response to a decline in the issues. Much of the responsibility for the selection of this recreative reading was entrusted personally to Folkard, for, as this councillor went on to say, the committee had 'the uttermost confidence in the discretion which was exercised by their excellent librarian, and he could give the public the assurance that the novels were most carefully selected by him, and the unsavoury yellow-backs as well as the penny dreadfuls were both conspicuous by their absence from the shelves'.

Around the turn of the century, Wigan too developed a network of delivery stations. Although the number of issues was much lower than in Blackburn, fiction remained by far the largest proportion, representing 80% in 1907 and 95% by 1914.

However, the continuing neglect of the lending library inevitably led to a serious decline in its use, which became most marked in the period between 1910 and 1914 when the annual issue fell from 87,000 to 55,000.

Crisis provoked by shortage of fiction

Folkard's initial reaction to the catastrophic decline in the issue was to dismiss it as of little consequence. He attributed the drop between 1910 and 1911 to the excellence of the reference library, and he also added that, as the largest proportionate decrease was in the fiction issue, this was not particularly significant. A further decrease in 1912 was again reported to be mainly in the issue of novels and was not, according to Folkard, a serious matter 'when we take into consideration the large increase of a better class of books in the Reference Library'.[48] However, the further loss of almost 20,000 issues between 1912 and 1913 could neither be ignored nor easily dismissed. The cause of this massive drop was the virtual abandonment of the purchase of new books, including novels, the annual report noting that only 44 books had been added.[49] This provoked a crisis both in the library committee and at the full town council, where a member of the library committee had to admit that the report was 'not very pleasant reading', and claimed the decline had been caused by insufficient funding.[50] Most of the novels in the lending library were reported to be in a dilapidated and dirty condition and unfit for public use; readers had, according to Folkard, been forced to resort either to the commercial circulating libraries or to the new cheap cinemas. The message to Folkard and the library committee was clear: the long-standing ideological concentration on the development of the reference library and upon the building of a reference stock of a far higher standard than was actually required by the public had been at the expense of a general neglect of the lending department and a loss of public appeal. The failure to address properly the demand for recreational books finally placed the library in a critically serious predicament, and, as Folkard himself noted in the library's annual report, 'I fear that the damage which is being done in this respect will take years to repair if something is not done during the next year to put this department upon a proper up-to-date footing.' The lending department issue fell again between 1913–1914, although this time by only a slight amount. Folkard claimed, probably with some truth, that this was in part due to the outbreak of war. He also commented, however, upon the inadequacy of the stock, which was in fact the main reason for the loss of the department's appeal; the issues, he said:

> 'ought to be four times as large as they are; the reason they are not is to be attributed to the general state of the stock of books, seventy-five per cent of which are either out-of-date or too dirty for circulation. To bring this department to a proper state of efficiency in accordance with modern methods and principles, the whole of the stock will require overhauling and renewing.[51]

The immediate remedial step was the purchase of 685 new titles for the lending department, over half of which were novels, and, as was hoped, the issues once again began to rise.[52] In the following years, a number of changes were implemented in the lending library; among them, the open access system and the shelving of books in author order rather than in a numerical order, both of which offered the public far better access to the library's novels.

The Wigan library committee

As was the case in Blackburn, the treatment of fiction in Wigan was primarily determined by the library committee. The political and economic profile of this committee bears marked similarities with Blackburn's, although there are also some notable differences. Wigan was a parliamentary and municipal Conservative stronghold; the town returned Conservative Members of Parliament throughout the entire period of the library's history discussed in this book; the town council too was ruled by the Conservatives, so much so that one recent historian has described Wigan as 'an almost perfect example of the Tory working-class area'.[53] Most council committees were accordingly dominated by the Conservatives, including the library committee, which had among its members Walter Mayhew, chairman of the Orrell Coal and Cannel Company, and Nathaniel ffarington Eckersley, a major Wigan cotton manufacturer. The library committee, which had no museum or art gallery to administer, was exceptionally large; its 1881 version, for example, consisted of 14 elected and 20 coopted members, very few of whom were non-conformist or Liberal. Indeed, the majority of the coopted members were Conservative businessmen or Anglican clergymen, a pattern which not infrequently provoked what the *Wigan Examiner* described as an 'annual squabble over the appointment of the Library Committee'.[54] Many members were coopted for social reasons rather than for literary or technical expertise and were not deeply committed to their role; of the 37 members of the 1888 committee 13 never attended a meeting, and nine attended less than three meetings. Towering over the library committee was the presence of Lord Lindsay, Wigan's leading industrialist and landowner, coopted member and chairman of the committee, who was made a freeman of Wigan in 1900 in recognition of his services to Wigan library. His obituary in the *Wigan Observer* noted that his numerous donations to the reference library had been undertaken in an attempt to 'try to make it worthy of a great place in the Library roll of this kingdom',[55] and it was principally through Lindsay that Folkard was appointed.

The members of the Wigan library committee were drawn largely from the town's economic and political elite, and shared considerable homogeneity of interest beyond the sphere of the public library's affairs. These common interests were founded upon the political, economic and social networks of which members, and indeed the librarian, were a part. Both Lindsay and Folkard were prominent Freemasons, as were other committee members, and the library contained an extensive collection of masonic books. Table 6.5 shows how the three most prominent committee members and the librarian met in social and professional circles

Table 6.5   Membership of social networks of library managers

	Lindsay	Folkard	Eckersley	Campbell
Library Committee	*	*	*	*
Conservative Party	*			*
Freemasons	*	*	*	*
Volunteer Rifles		*	*	
Industrial connections	*		*	*
The Library Association	*	*		*

These relationships and common interests formed social bonds between those responsible for the management of the library. Lindsay and Folkard in particular had strong ties, sharing common interests in Freemasonry, bibliographical scholarship, The Library Association and the development of a scientific and reference-orientated public library service.

The major difference between Wigan and Blackburn was that, in Wigan, the reference department was all-important, and what happened in the lending department was not taken seriously until the crisis provoked by its neglect forced the committee to recognize this as an error and to acknowledge the necessity of fiction to the survival of the library. This acceptance of fiction was in keeping with other aspects of recreational provision for the working classes in Wigan, both Lindsay and Eckersley being well-known for their contributions to this. For example, Lindsay frequently organized picnics at Haigh Hall, his estate on the outskirts of Wigan, which were attended by up to 8,000 visitors. While fiction may not have been enthusiastically promoted, it was nevertheless tolerated as a necessary adjunct to a public library service. However, the ideological conviction of the library committee and the librarian that the role of the public library was to provide a reference and information service of the highest possible technical standard with little regard to public demand or community need proved to be mistaken. The standard of reference service in Wigan was far beyond the level required by the local community and, because this standard was achievable only by ignoring the community demand for popular fiction and an improved lending library, it could not be sustained.

NOTES AND REFERENCES TO CHAPTER 6

1   Kelly, T., *A history of public libraries in Great Britain 1845–1975*, Library Association, 1977, 44–5.
2   Cowell, P., 'Experientia docet; or, the thoughts and experiences of a public librarian', *Library chronicle*, **5**, 1888, 155–66.
3   Bramwell, W. S., *Reminiscences of a public librarian: a retrospective view*, Preston, 1916, 42.
4   McAllister, J. Y. L., 'New ways of keeping down the issues of fiction', *Library*, **6**, 1894, 236–7.
5   Elliott, G., 'Our readers and what they read', *Library*, **7**, 1895, 276–81.
6   Aldred, T., 'Discursive jottings on novels', *Library world*, **2**, 1899–1900, 295–8.
7   *Library Association record*, 1908, 401.
8   Greenwood, T., 'The great fiction question', *Libraries, Museums and Art Galleries yearbook*, 1897, 97–116.
9   Ingram, J., 'A day's reading in the Mitchell Library', Glasgow, *Library*,

1, 1889, 281–92.

10 Edwards, E., *Free town libraries*, Trubner, 1869, 46.

11 Taylor, F., 'In defence of fiction reading', *Library world*, 1, 1898, 113–6.

12 Cowell, op. cit., ref. 2.

13 *Manchester Guardian*, 24 September 1909.

14 *Library Association record*, 2, 1900, 27–8.

15 Dunne, T., *A history of public libraries in Bolton from the beginnings to 1974*, Unpublished PhD thesis, University of Strathclyde, 1981.

16 'Presidential address to The Library Association', *Library chronicle*, 4, 1887, 129–35.

17 *Northern Daily Telegraph*, 11 April 1906.

18 Greenwood, op.cit., ref. 8.

19 *Blackburn Times*, 24 November 1894.

20 Blackburn Free Library and Museum, *Minutes*, 16 May 1877.

21 Blackburn Free Library, *Annual report*, 1862–63.

22 Blackburn Free Library, *Annual report*, 1863–64.

23 Blackburn Free Library, *Annual report*, 1864–65.

24 Blackburn Free Library, *Annual report*, 1866–67.

25 Blackburn Free Library, *Annual report*, 1866–67.

26 Blackburn Free Library, *Annual report*, 1868–69.

27 Blackburn Free Library, *Annual report*, 1868–69.

28 Blackburn Free Library, *Annual report*, 1870–71.

29 Blackburn Free Library, *Annual report*, 1869–70.

30 *Blackburn Times*, 1 March 1890.

31 Blackburn Free Library, *Annual report*, 1892–92.

32 *Preston Herald*, 21 June 1890.

33 *Blackburn Standard*, 15 April 1893.

34 *Blackburn Standard*, 22 April 1893.

35 Blackburn Free Library, *Annual report*, 1897–98.

36 Blackburn Free Library, *Annual report*, 1901–02.

37 Blackburn Free Library, *Annual report*, 1906–07.

38 *Blackburn Times*, 14 December 1867.

39 *Blackburn Year book*, 1902.

40 *Blackburn Year book*, 1909.

41 Storch, R. D., 'Introduction: persistence and change in nineteenth century popular culture', in Storch, R. D. (ed.), *Popular culture and custom in nineteenth century England*, Croom Helm, 1982, 1–19.

42 Joyce, P., *Work, society and politics. The culture of the factory in later Victorian England*, Methuen, 1982.

43 Poole, R., *Popular leisure and the music hall in nineteenth century Bolton*, Centre for North-West Regional Studies, University of Lancaster,

Occasional Paper no. 12, 1982.

44   Connor, S., *The long march: a study of working-class politics in Blackburn from December 1883 to January 1906*, Unpublished dissertation, Ruskin College, 1988.

45   Abram, W., 'Social condition and political prospects of the Lancashire workmen', *Fortnightly review*, 4, 1868, 426–41.

46   Wigan Public Library, *Annual report*, 1889.

47   *Wigan Observer*, 4 March 1898.

48   Wigan Public Library, *Annual report*, 1913.

49   Wigan Public Library, *Annual report*, 1914.

50   *Wigan Observer*, 5 March 1914.

51   Wigan Public Library, *Annual report*, 1915.

52   Wigan Public Library, *Annual report*, 1916.

53   Brown, D., *Coalopolis: a history of Wigan*, Wigan, 198–.

54   *Wigan Examiner*, 14 November 1894.

55   *Wigan Observer*, 4 February 1913.

Chapter 7

Uplifting Reading: The Public Library and the Civic Gospel

W hile some public libraries were prepared, for whatever reason, to provide popular fiction in response to demand, others adopted a more discerning approach. By the early years of the twentieth century, the fiction debate was less, if at all, about whether libraries should provide novels, but, in the words of Ernest Baker,[1] about whether libraries 'had the right, and should exercise the right, to shut out any species of novel for which there is a popular demand'.

The assumption that popularity was in some way incompatible with worth is revealing, and Baker's conclusion was that libraries did indeed have such a right, and that the recreation they ought to provide was not the undemanding and passive form of reading romances or adventure stories, but a more culturally elite experience as offered by the National Gallery, Kew Gardens and the British Museum. To judge from the professional press, many librarians shared this view, but were individually and collectively powerless to realise it because their committees placed a higher priority on popularizing the library and consequently provided novels in bulk. However, some library committees perceived a primary duty not to provide a community-orientated recreational service but to promote fiction of literary merit and to direct popular reading patterns, persuasively or coercively. Such committees had few qualms in assuming the role of cultural gatekeeper, and public libraries provided idealistic committees with singular opportunities for the implementation of their values and beliefs. The development of the public library service in the small Lancashire cotton town of Darwen illustrates the ways in which a library committee with a clear set of values and a strong sense of mission used the library as an agency for the control of popular reading.

THE CIVIC GOSPEL IN DARWEN

Darwen is situated five miles to the south of Blackburn, and like its near neighbour grew rapidly in the nineteenth century, although by 1901 its population was still a comparatively modest 38,000. Its relatively small size and its location in a steep-sided valley with restricted communications contributed to a close-knit community which was governed by a small but influential economic and political elite. Unlike Blackburn, Darwen had a flourishing literary culture which was most notably evident in the town's Literary Society, a predominantly middle-class institution to which most of the library committee belonged.

The distinctive features of local government in Darwen in the later nineteenth and early twentieth century were the hegemony of the Liberal Party and the domination of the town council by non-conformists, more specifically by Congregationalists. There was a manifest sense of civic duty in the council's undertakings, based on the belief that it had a wider obligation than a basic provision of material facilities. This missionary approach was neatly expressed by the borough librarian, Joseph Pomfret, in the town's fiftieth anniversary souvenir brochure, which he dedicated to the youth of the town in the hope that 'they will obtain a clearer idea of their civic inheritance – particularly of what has been done for the public since 1878 – and that it will help them to realise the importance of local government not only to the collective unit – the community – but also in the life of every individual citizen'.[2] The underlying principle of the civic gospel was that municipal authorities had a duty to care for the moral as well as the physical well-being of their communities. It has been described by Asa Briggs as a 'whole civic philosophy',[3] and was commonly found in local government in the last century, being particularly associated with non-conformist/Liberal councils.

The civic gospel originated in Birmingham in the mid-nineteenth century in the non-conformist ideal of practised Christianity preached by George Dawson and later by Robert Dale, and in the Liberal politics personified in Joseph Chamberlain, Birmingham's mayor between 1873 and 1876. A town council had, in the words of George Dawson, a duty to its inhabitants comparable to that of a nation towards its citizens: a corporation should be like a church, providing for the physical and social welfare of its community under the missionary inspiration of the gospel. As an illustration of this, Dawson suggested that the public library movement was an almost perfect example, likening it to the 'largest and widest Church ever established' as it placed no restrictions on entry or membership and transcended existing economic and social differences. Birmingham's library was, he said, '. . . an expression of a conviction . . . that a town like this exists for moral and intellectual purposes ... the Corporation of a borough like this has every function to discharge that is discharged by the master of a household'.[4]

Robert Dale, a prominent Congregationalist minister, urged Congregationalists to become involved in public affairs and identified their specific responsibilities in the realm of popular leisure; they had a duty to become '. . . Aldermen and Town Councillors. They ought to see to it that there are good schools for every class of the population; that there are harmless public amusements'.[5] Dale, who was also a Liberal, said there was not a duality but a convergence of religion and the requirements of the State, epitomized in his belief that to hold municipal or political office was in fact to act as a Minister of God.[6]

Through its domination by Liberals and Congregationalists, Darwen's council chamber provided a seed-bed in which the culture of the civic gospel flourished. The contribution of Darwen's Congregationalists to the implementation of the civic gospel in the town's municipal service was remarkable, and extended well into the present century. By 1962, one Congregational church alone had provided the town with ten of its mayors. Their influence upon the management of the public library was profound; in 1903, one church included in its congregation not only five members of the library committee but the borough librarian as well. By 1914, there were nine Congregational churches in Darwen, making it by far the largest of the non-conformist denominations, and the most influential members of the Darwen library committee all attended one of these. However, the influence of Congregationalism extended beyond the council chamber into other spheres of civic life, such as the Darwen Literary Society and the local circle of the National Home Reading Union. In common with members of all non-conformist denominations, Congregationalists took an active interest in the provision of rational recreational opportunities, and most churches organized a wide range of leisure-time activities, such as sewing circles, Pleasant Sunday Afternoons, discussion groups, Bands of Hope, excursions, picnics and sports. Recreational reading was particularly important and it is worth noting that the Religious Tract Society, which published an immense number of instructive and moral novels throughout the nineteenth century was founded by a Congregationalist minister, George Burder, in 1799. The virtues of systematic and constructive reading were much extolled, and the potential of public libraries in providing suitable recreational reading was highly valued, illustrated in a 1907 church magazine's idealistic picture of readers flocking to the library:

> [it was] delightful on the evening after the holidays to see the Public Library crowded with eager book selectors . . . The healthful interest in life, which carries so many of our citizens so far a-field during our holiday season, finds increasingly its counterpart in their desire to widen their acquaintance with our literature, and the still larger world of fact and fiction which it opens up to them.[7]

Library practice and the civic gospel in Darwen

From the beginning, Darwen operated an innovative library service. It was, when its library opened in 1871, the first non-incorporated town to adopt the Libraries Acts, and in 1908 its new Carnegie-sponsored library building was designed specifically to facilitate open access and also housed a lecture theatre. The library was typical of the period; there was a good stock of technical books, but always a larger stock of literary and popular novels, and the majority of the members were drawn from the lower middle and working classes. More novels were borrowed than of any other class of literature, and, as was customary, book selection was undertaken by the library committee.

Until the mid-1890s, the progress of the library was relatively unexceptional. However, in 1895, Darwen introduced open access, at that time being only the third library in the country to do so, and this marked the beginning of a period of approximately 15 years in which there was a remarkable growth of active interest in the promotion of the reading and borrowing of literary fiction and standard novels. The inspiration for the introduction of open access clearly originated in the committee, for the librarian, Cawthorne, recorded that he had been instructed by the chairman of the committee to visit Clerkenwell public library to evaluate the open access system there.[8] Because Darwen was the first library in the north of England to adopt open access, it was frequently contacted by neighbouring libraries in which open access was being considered. Several of the queries received were directly concerned with the potential effect of open access upon fiction issues; as Darwen's librarian responded to a query from the Accrington library committee about the relationship between open access and fiction issues: 'Our fiction issues compare favourably with other libraries, which makes me think that the Open Access system which is in use at Darwen, may be the cause. Borrowers taking a glance at the books in the History or Science classes very often [choose] a book from these shelves in place of a novel'.[9]

Whether this was in fact true is open to question, for few libraries were prepared to admit that open access had increased fiction borrowing, and everyone associated with or employed by Darwen library adhered to this official line. Ralph Yates, the chairman of the library committee and an enthusiastic supporter of open access, believed that instead of increasing the fiction issue, it was more likely to reduce it. There is, however, some doubt as to the veracity of these claims, as one of Darwen's librarians, after taking a post in another authority, claimed that open access had made borrowers less purposive, lowered staff morale and had in fact increased the fiction issue. Indeed, it seems more likely that open access increased the tendency to borrow fiction, for, as a *Darwen Gazette* journalist noted in 1908, a walk around the library shelves revealed a stock of historical and scientific books practically untouched, but 'aching voids' in the fiction section; most of the books that were out, he reported, reached only a 'low level of mediocrity'.[10] The relevant fact remains however, that the library committee wished to promote the reading of literary fiction and believed that open access would assist this.

The censorship of popular novels

At the time that Darwen introduced open access, there was an ample supply of popular novels in the library – the catalogue indicates 67 copies of 56 titles by Mary Braddon, 20 copies of 20 titles by James Payn and 56 copies of 31 titles by Mrs Henry Wood – and the issues of fiction were substantial. Unlike James Duff Brown's archetypal library committee, Darwen's committee had a high degree of literary expertise as many of its members belonged to the Darwen Literary Society, and its book selection sub-committees had, over the years, added many standard novels to complement the more popular tales and romances. The committee's approach is typified in the fact that when borrowers were allowed an extra 'student' ticket which entitled them to more than the normal number of books, this was conditional upon the title chosen being a non-fiction work or one from the 'higher classes of literature'. However, in 1901, the committee chairman, Ralph Yates, devised and implemented a strategy to reduce the provision and borrowing of popular fiction. In February of that year Yates gave a paper to the Darwen Literary Society,[11] in which he spoke about patterns of fiction borrowing and his concern about the extent of the demand for and supply of popular tales and romances which accounted for 84% of the issue. Fiction was, he said, damaging to the image of the library. The task of the book selection sub-committee was becoming increasingly difficult because of the growth in publishing output, six new novels being published for every working day of the year. As if testing the water, he referred to the British Museum's practice of keeping new novels in reserve for five years, and suggested that if a similar time-scale for the purchase of novels were adopted in Darwen, it would avoid the acquisition of many worthless books, though he did add that exceptions to such a procedure would have to be made in the case of novels of 'undoubted repute', which would be identified by the selection committee. He insisted that his thoughts were hypothetical as the library committee were 'not censors, and it is a nice point as to what limits should be imposed upon their discretion'. Despite this assurance, the library committee decided, within a matter of weeks, that newly published popular novels would no longer be purchased. Yates reported the committee's decision to the town council unapologetically:

The library committee intended to make a stand against buying any book simply because it was asked for. It was the deliberate act of the committee to retrench in this direction. Any book of approved standard will be found there, but the prevailing novel of the day, the puerile trash that was simply the craze of the moment, would not be found at any rate for the ensuing 12 months.[12]

He was fully aware of the controversial nature of this move, explaining it to the local press on the grounds of economic prudence, but was nevertheless obliged to admit that the library committee had effectively established itself as judge of what the public should read:

The novel reader of the present time was not the person who appreciated Dickens, Thackeray and George Elliott [sic.]. Against the novel of today the Library Committee were prepared to make a stand ... if the people of Darwen cried out, he wanted them to know that the absence of such and such a book was the deliberate act of the committee. Any book which was of approved reputation and deserving of a place on the shelves would be found there. But the novel of the present day – the silly and puerile trash – will not be found there.[13]

Reactions to the ban on the purchase of popular fiction

There was a mixed reaction to Darwen's censorship of popular novels. Strong support came from literary circles and the library profession. The local journalist, Nicholas Chadwick, who, like Yates, was a Congregationalist and a member of the Darwen Literary Society, supported the committee's decision:[14]

. . . it is one of the leading characteristics of novel readers that they are always after some new thing. The newer the novel the better, quite irrespective of whether it has any literary merits, about which they rarely trouble themselves. It scarcely occurs to them that the keener the demand the greater the temptation to manufacture an inferior article, but that is precisely what is taking place in the literary world, especially with regard to fiction. No wonder that the Free Library Committee feel themselves no longer justified in spending any large amount of their funds upon what they very justly call 'silly and puerile trash' which characterises so large a proportion of the novels of the present day. Of course it will be generally understood that the Committee do not refuse to buy works of fiction, but what they stipulate is that any such purchases in future shall not be made to satisfy any mere passing whim or caprice, but must be a work of 'approved reputation and worthy of a place upon the shelves of the Library'.

To long-suffering librarians accustomed to working for committees interested only in the popularization of the library, Darwen's course provided a welcome lead to be followed, and the *Library world* described the decision as 'heroic', criticizing only the proposed delay of one year which should, it said, have been ten![15]

Beyond literary and professional circles, the decision received a critical and hostile response. Even the normally supportive Liberal *Darwen News* expressed its reservations, commenting 'How the readers of light literature will regard this movement we do not know, but we are pretty confident that it will not find much favour in the town generally . . . is it wise that the requirements of the few should be supplied to the detriment of the reading public?'[16] The Conservative *Darwen Gazette*, which habitually criticized the library and its committee, published a lengthier column which defended the right of working people to read popular novels for leisure and launched a personal attack upon the library committee:

> Who are the majority of the people who go for books? Working folks who go simply to find something to pass the leisure hours in a pleasant way. They have no burning wish for culture, or to acquire literary precision. They pay rates either directly or indirectly to secure the book they want, but here are a body of gentlemen who are taking the initiative of refusing to give it to them. .
>
> They sigh for men and women who will read novels that live, and not those that are born, blossom and languish in a few month's time. How many novels are there that do live? Are there two in a year? If so, are the Library Committee going to confine themselves to the purchase of these two, and leave all the others out of account? Is there no profit to be found in reading Hall Caine, Guy Boothby, Thomas Hardy, Hitchen, Annie S. Swan, Rose Carey and others? Probably Councillor Yates will answer 'No' and judged by the canons of style and other mystic formalities by which the cult of Frederic Harrison judge these things, Councillor Yates is probably right, but judged by the standard that a free library is for the purpose of providing pleasant recreation to working people in their hours of leisure, the answer will probably be 'No'.[17]

The public reaction is difficult to gauge, but correspondence in local newspapers gave little credence to the alleged economic rationale for the restriction on novels, which was perceived as a lame excuse, and defended the use of the public library for simple non-utilitarian leisure:

> When I have done my work I like a book which has plenty of action about it, something that will keep me interested, and I care more for 'go' in the plot than I do for beautifully constructed sentences. My favourite authors

are those who, like Boothby, Weyman, Castle and Max Pemberton can keep me interested in the stories they tell. Probably my taste will appear poor and uncultivated by the refined tastes of Mr. Ralph Yates, but the difficulty I have in securing the volumes I like and their well-thumbed condition when I do get them shows me that my taste is not much different from that of the majority of the users of the Library . . . perhaps because I do not agree with Mr. Yates' ideas I may be lacking in intellectual culture. If Mr. Yates is going to try the experiment of making everybody's taste agree with his own, and of buying only what he considers to be literature, he can write it down that he has taken the first step to make the Library unpopular.[18]

Resentment of the committee's cultural elitism and interference with working-class leisure is evident in another letter:

It is, I know, like flying in the face of destiny to suggest to the members of the Darwen Free Library that there is anything really good among the fiction of the popular novel writers of the day. They have through their chairman proclaimed open hostility to the productions of the men who are the craze of the moment . . . one may well ask, not whether this novel or that novel is worth buying, but rather who has constituted the few members of the Library Committee as the judges of what is or what is not readable? Reading is a matter of taste, and the ordinary working man and working woman prefers the novel for his or her leisure to any other kind of book. The average person who likes a bit of reading on Sundays has neither the time nor the inclination to develop a literary faculty, what is wanted is an easy pleasurable bit of fiction. The Library Committee say no! We will give you something higher; go to Dickens, Thackeray, Scott, and others. The average man and woman turn their backs on such talk, and buy a pennyworth of fiction from the newsagent.[19]

It is difficult to evaluate the success of this censorship as some new novels continued to be added to the library, and, after the first wave of outrage, the public reaction became somewhat muted. The local Liberal newspaper, the *Darwen News*, overcame its initial reservations about the scheme and was eventually to describe the policy as an investment in the educational and moral standard of the people, the benefits of which would not be visible immediately.[20] Yates remained bullish about the committee's action and claimed in a letter to the *Manchester Guardian* that the issue of works by standard novelists had increased since the implementation of the policy, although this is hardly surprising in view of the fact that works of popular fiction were now in shorter supply, and conceded that the committee had exercised censorship:

Singular to say, this revival received a great impetus by the adoption of our Committee of a rigorous policy of censorship, which was widely commented upon by the Press at the time, and in some cases severely criticized. The simple test we apply, as far as practicable, in all novels before purchase, is this – Does the book possess literary merit and a healthy tone? If not, it is simply consigned to the dust heap of oblivion, whither such quantities of similar trash have preceded it.[21]

The practice of not buying new popular fiction was adhered to for a considerable period of time, but was gradually relaxed, without publicity, and without being recorded in the library minutes. Yates eventually admitted that the committee's standards had perhaps been too idealistic, and explained that an upturn in the library's economic circumstances allowed a more relaxed approach to book buying. By 1905, the fiction issue stood at 57.6% and was soon to reach over 60%, a proportion which was maintained until 1914. The long-term effect on the popularity of fiction in the library was minimal, although the local debate about the provision of fiction in the town library continued to smoulder until the outbreak of war.

Extension activities to improve popular reading

In addition to the restrictive measures described above, there was a range of initiatives to persuade readers to turn from popular fiction to literary fiction and non-fiction. In nearly all cases, these were devised and implemented by the library committee collectively or by its members individually, the librarian being a facilitator rather than an originator. In some instances, there were close links with other organizations with a vested interest in the promotion of literature, notably the Darwen Literary Society. If these initiatives were undertaken with the aim of educating working-class readers, then they were at best only partially successful because many of the programmes were organized by the middle classes and attended by the middle classes; apart from the library lectures which are described in the following paragraph, working-class readers were, in most places, notable only for their absence.

Library lectures

One of the first measures to improve popular reading patterns was the provision of library lectures, which were organized in 1901 to coincide with the restrictions on fiction purchase. These were advertized under the more appealing description of 'half hour talks', and initially proved to be so popular that they were usually over-subscribed. Their purpose was, in the words of the then librarian, Walter Rae, to promote the circulation of good and valuable literature, and to encourage the members of the library to read something other than popular fiction.[22] Yates, too, was enthusiastic about the lectures, which were intended to 'awaken fresh interest in, and to create a stimulus for that which is best and most wholesome in our literature . . . among all classes a vast amount of time is wasted on profitless reading'.[23] The local press welcomed the introduction of the lectures, commenting on the need to correct the 'misuse' of the library as a storehouse of fiction. The second series of lectures moved away from the topics of local interest which had characterized the first series to concentrate on the benefits of systematic reading, but average attendances dropped to 70. Nevertheless, the library committee remained unperturbed: the lectures might not be well attended, but they were, according to Yates, 'doing good' because they promoted the reading of literary and standard novels. Many lectures were delivered by members of the library committee, the topics of these including Shakespeare's King Henry VIII, Thackeray, and Macaulay.

The National Home Reading Union in Darwen

The major initiative to encourage the reading of literary fiction occurred through the library's involvement with the National Home Reading Union, a voluntary body whose purpose was to promote systematic and improving reading. The history of the National Home Reading Union is described in Chapter 8, but it is significant, in view of the circumstances in Darwen, that it was founded by John Brown Paton, a prominent Congregationalist, and its denominational origins must have been an influential factor in its favourable reception among the members of the Darwen committee. The National Home Reading Union's *modus operandi* was to encourage the establishment of local reading circles which met under the direction of a leader to read and discuss set books. In the early years of the twentieth century, the Union instigated cooperative work with a number of public libraries in the hope that libraries would coordinate local circles as a means of promoting the reading of books other than popular novels and tales.

A National Home Reading Union circle had existed in Darwen since the mid-1890s, though this was not formally connected to the library. This had met fortnightly, but had been at least as much a middle-class social gathering as a self-improvement group. Darwen library became a member of the National Home Reading Union in 1905, the *Darwen News* commenting in approval that:

> To supply books is not, or should not be, the sole aim of our public library. It has other and higher duties to perform, and one of the most important is

for its officers to guide individuals and societies as to how to read and what to read. This brings us to a point very similar to the aims of the National Home Reading Union.[24]

The following week, Walter Rae, then the serving borough librarian, wrote to the paper to publicize the beginnings of the library's links with the Union, suggesting that the proposed reading circles would not only provide a recreational alternative to the town's billiards and cards clubs but would nurture Darwen's future civic and social leaders. The establishment of a library-based circle took some time, partly through lack of a venue and partly through the fact that no one volunteered to lead it. A circle was finally established in 1908, when a member of the library committee agreed to act as leader, and, after a preliminary lecture to introduce the Union and its aims, weekly meetings were arranged for Friday evenings in the library. Each session began with an introductory lecture designed to generate enthusiasm for reading and at the first meeting the books or subjects to be studied were chosen by the circle; these included Ruskin's *Unto this last*, Eliot's *Adam Bede*, Watt's *Geology for beginners* and Jevons' *Political economy*. There was a local charge of sixpence to cover the cost of the carriage of the books from the Union's headquarters and of an occasional lantern lecture. Only a dozen people joined the initial circle, thus dashing any hopes the committee may have held in terms of reaching a mass popular readership. Membership did expand in the following years, reaching 44 in 1910, but remaining well below a level that could be claimed as significant.

A further initiative to encourage the reading of literary fiction was the launch of the quarterly *Darwen Public Library journal* in 1902, which, in Yates' words, aimed to create a 'taste for reading books of a better class than the ordinary novel'.[25]

The library committee and the control of fiction

The treatment of fiction in Darwen library was markedly different from that in Blackburn and Wigan, as indeed was the library's whole approach to popular reading. The important feature, however, is that it was determined by the library committee. In comparison with library committees in other towns, Darwen's was relatively small, with a limited number of coopted members, and functioned efficiently as a homogeneous body. It comprised, on average, between 13 and 16 members, and thus embodied Greenwood's ideal of a 'small working committee, the members of which attend to their duties',[26] and was extremely active in the management of the library and the organization of extension activities. Its notable features were: its low rate of turnover, which resulted in some members remaining on the committee for over 30 years; its overall control by the Liberals; the presence of a high proportion of Congregationalists and the fact that many members were also active members of the Darwen Literary Society.

The committee combined a mixture of economic power, Congregationalism and a belief in the importance of literary culture, personified in its influential chairman, Ralph Yates, who was educated in Congregational schools in Darwen, established his own business as a cotton waste merchant, was elected to the council as a Liberal, became an active member of the town's principal Congregational church, and was also a founder member and later president of the Darwen Literary Society. As a local paper noted:

> it was not difficult to see that he had been no casual student of literature, but one who had explored the whole field and stored away many of its choice gems . . . In appointing him Chairman of the Free Library Committee, the Council showed its appreciation of his undoubted literary abilities, and it would certainly have been difficult to have found a man more eminently suited to the position. Equally difficult, we imagine, would it have been to have found Mr. Yates a post more congenial to his tastes and inclinations.[27]

Although Yates clearly possessed charismatic appeal, the power of the library committee was structurally linked to that of the town and council, and its treatment of fiction was a reflection of the local ideology of Congregationalism and the civic gospel. Other prominent members of the committee included Timothy Lightbown, a cotton manufacturer, Liberal, Congregationalist and founder member of the Darwen Literary Society; Nathaniel Jepson, a Congregationalist, temperance organizer, founder member of the Darwen Literary Society and owner of a personal library of 5,000 volumes, and Ernest Morgan Davies, a cotton manufacturer, Congregationalist and Liberal. The number of coopted members was kept to a minimum, and, unlike Wigan, such members were invited to join the committee for their literary expertise rather than as a mark of social favour. Coopted members were almost invariably Congregationalists and members of the Literary Society.

Just as Freemasonry provided a social forum beyond the council chambers for the Wigan library committee, the Literary Society served a similar function in Darwen, a major difference being that the Literary Society had a clear association of interest in the provision of fiction in the library. The Society was formed in 1882 and became a thriving association which combined literary interests with a lively social programme. There was an extensive overlap between membership of the library committee and the Literary Society, and committee members and serving librarians frequently delivered papers to the Society. It is not difficult to imagine the embarrassment caused to such committee men by the library's image as a purveyor of sensational novels and romances, particularly as so many of the discussions organized by the Literary Society featured critical attacks on popular fiction and its reading.

Darwen's Congregationalist community constituted a further element in the network through which committee members shared common values and made personal contacts. Table 7.1 shows how membership of the library committee was closely associated with that of the Darwen Literary Society and of the Congregational churches.

Table 7.1   Links between the Literary Society, the library, and the Congregationalist churches in Darwen

Literary Society President	Year	Library Committee	Congregationalist
James Dimmock	1882	No	Yes
J. Ballantyne	1886	Yes	Yes
F. G. Hindle	1887	Yes	Yes
E. M. Davies	1889	Yes	Yes
J. Williamson	1890	Yes	No
E. Schofield	1894	No	Yes
A. Carus	1895	Yes	No
R. Yates	1897	Yes	Yes
N. Jepson	1898	Yes	Yes
J. Leach	1899	No	Yes
T. Lightbown	1902	Yes	Yes
W. P. Kay	1906	Yes	Yes
T.E. Holgate	1908	Yes	No

The idealistic belief in the importance of literary culture combined with the Congregationalist creed of a civic gospel equipped the library committee with a mission to replace the reading of popular fiction with novels of a higher literary standard, and the lengthy periods of office served by most committee members contributed to a homogeneous and stable influence over the affairs of the library for many decades. The library service in Darwen effectively became an expression of the values of the library committee, which in effect were those of the town's political and economic elite, and the professional standards of the librarians were very much a secondary, if not indeed insignificant, force in comparison.

CONCLUSION

Perhaps the most significant feature of fiction provision in Darwen was not the committee's audacious attempt to control the availability of popular fiction, but the lack of success the scheme achieved. The reading public and the press were not prepared to tolerate what they perceived as censorship without some reaction. Even a number of years after the restrictions on the purchase of popular fiction a local newspaper reaffirmed the right of the reading public to expect libraries to provide novels simply for recreational purposes:

> It is very obvious that the masses of the people of Darwen prefer fiction to religious and philosophical literature. This is not difficult to understand. A working-class community naturally seeks relaxation and recreation in light literature as a change from their ordinary labour . . . Their tastes are a part of their nature, and we are not sure whether it is not possible for them to find as much elevating and wholesome food in the works of our great English story tellers as in perhaps the more inspiring literary efforts of the Divines.[28]

The overall campaign to improve reading patterns through the provision of lectures and National Home Reading Union circles did not meet with much success either; certainly there was no significant participation by working-class readers. This was largely due to the fact that many of these events were essentially middle-class social gatherings at which a working-class person would have felt uncomfortable, and is connected to the fact that Congregationalism, though committed to the civic gospel, had an essentially middle-class base.[29] The vision of a public library service with a leisure function related only to personal development, elite culture and educational advancement was not achievable in the face of public demand and support for a service which offered relaxation and simple entertainment.

NOTES AND REFERENCES TO CHAPTER 7

1   Baker, E., 'The standard of fiction in public libraries', *Library Association record*, 1907, 70–80.
2   Pomfret, J., *Official souvenir of the fiftieth anniversary of the incorporation of the Borough of Darwen*, 1928.
3   Briggs, A., *Victorian cities*, Penguin, 1968, 184.
4   Parsons, G. (ed.), *Religion in Victorian Britain. Volume three: Sources*, Manchester University Press, 1988, 296–300. See also: Jones, R. T., *Congregationalism in England 1662–1962*, Independent Press, 1962.
5   Quoted in: Hennock, E.P., *Fit and proper persons: ideal and reality in*

nineteenth century urban government, Arnold, 1973, 154–69.

6   Parsons, op. cit., ref. 4, 207.
7   *Duckworth St. Congregational Church Monthly Magazine*, August 1907.
8   Borough of Darwen, *Librarian's report book* [ms], January 1895.
9   *Darwen Library Letter Book 1891–1900*, 3 June 1899.
10   *Darwen Gazette*, 8 August 1908.
11   *Darwen News*, 13 February 1901.
12   *Darwen Gazette*, 8 June 1901.
13   *Darwen News*, 15 June 1901.
14   ibid.
15   *Library world*, 4, 1901–1902, 48.
16   *Darwen News*, 5 June 1901.
17   *Darwen Gazette*, 8 June 1901.
18   *Darwen Weekly Advertiser*, 21 June 1901.
19   *Darwen Gazette*, 2 August 1902.
20   *Darwen News*, 7 June 1902.
21   *Manchester Guardian*, 20 February 1903.
22   *Library world*, 5, 1903, 623–9.
23   *Darwen Gazette*, 16 February 1901.
24   *Darwen News*, 7 October 1905.
25   *Darwen Public Library Committee Agenda*, 24 November 1902.
26   Greenwood, T., *Public libraries*, Cassell, 4th edn, 1894, Chapter 17.
27   *Darwen News*, 31 October 1908; 6 October 1934.
28   *Darwen Gazette*, 17 March 1906.
29   Sutton, R., 'Congregationalism in its relation to the working class', *Lancashire congregational calendar*, 1887, 27–30.

Chapter 8

The National Home Reading Union

THE NATIONAL HOME READING UNION
AND SYSTEMATIC READING

An active middle-class interest in the improvement of popular leisure was one of the principal characteristics of rational recreation. This was usually of a voluntary nature, and involved members of the middle classes organizing recreational activities designed both to be an alternative to working-class pursuits and to promote a more harmonious relationship between the classes by bringing them together in a common recreational interest. The phrase 'rational recreation' was rarely used explicitly – although there was, in the mid-nineteenth century, a Leeds Rational Recreation Society – but this should not disguise the fact that a great deal of energy was invested in recreational provision of this sort, especially, as we have seen in the preceding chapters, by the temperance movement and the non-conformist churches. Many organizations from these backgrounds developed an interest in recreational reading, but, on a national scale, the work of the National Home Reading Union represented a major attempt to improve popular reading on the rational recreation model.

The National Home Reading Union was founded by the Congregationalist minister John Brown Paton in 1889, with the objective of encouraging a profitable use of leisure time through the promotion of systematic and improving reading. Bearing many of the hallmarks of mid-nineteenth century rational recreation, though separated from this by several decades, the origins of the National Home Reading Union lay in the increased concern about popular recreational reading which followed the Education Act 1870 and the growth of the reading public and mass commercial publishing. The history of the Union provides further evidence of the importance of non-conformist religion, particularly Congregationalism, in the development and provision of leisure facilities and opportunities.

John Brown Paton was born into a Congregationalist family in Ayrshire in 1830, and trained as an Independent minister at Springhill College in Birmingham, where he was a fellow student of Robert W. Dale, whose view that recreation should essentially be a morally uplifting activity Paton shared, and was later to promote actively. In 1854, Paton obtained a post as a Congregationalist minister in Sheffield and then, in 1863, became the first principal of the Congregational Institute in Nottingham, from where he devoted much of the remainder of his life to the encouragement of rational and improving leisure pursuits for working-class people. Like many nineteenth-century leisure reformers Paton was especially concerned by the effect of urban leisure facilities, particularly public houses, on home life and family cohesion, although he readily understood why the public house might seem more attractive than the public library where 'all talking is forbidden'.[1] In contrast to work, which imposed control and conformity, urban leisure introduced to working-class lives a potentially dangerous mixture of freedom and choice; as Paton observed: '. . . it is the evening social, leisure life of the people which is the most important in forming moral habit and character . . . we have not yet realised the importance of these social hours, the necessity of filling them brightly and recreatively, so as to quicken the intelligence and elevate taste'.[2] Paton was deeply impressed by Walter Besant's novel *All sorts and conditions of men*,[3] in which Besant described a People's Palace which would provide rational amusement for working people with little alternative access to elevating or useful leisure activities. Inspired by Besant's vision of the role that leisure could play in promoting the moral well-being of society, and enthused by the Congregationalist ideal of rational Christian recreation, Paton became instrumental in the formation of numerous agencies for the promotion of improving leisure activities, among them the Recreative Evening Schools Association in 1885, the Cooperative Holiday Association in 1892 and the Boys' and Girls' League of Honour in 1906. However, it was through his specific concern about the link between the conduct of youth and the lack of moral standard in much popular literature that he developed an interest in establishing a similar sort of organization to achieve an improvement in popular reading. It is in this context of leisure reform and rational recreation, infused by Congregationalist idealism, that the development and work of the National Home Reading Union are best evaluated.

The evolution of the National Home Reading Union

The principal objective of the National Home Reading Union was to encourage and promote the systematic reading of morally and educationally improving literature. In adopting this aim, it was simply realizing a long-standing ambition of many middle-class readers in converting reading from a pastime to an improving, serviceable and wholesome intellectual occupation. Its chief method for achieving this was the promotion of local reading circles. However, it must be noted that these were not a new concept, for before widespread literacy books and newspapers were often read aloud in public. As early as 1858, HMI Reverend Brookfield had suggested the benefits of small societies for public reading where working-class people could, for a nominal fee, hear books read aloud 'not so much to instruct as simply to amuse'. Brookfield, together with Charles Plumptre, established an experimental programme of recreational reading circles in London under the auspices of a Public Reading Society; admission was sixpence for those who could afford it, a penny for others.[4] The first reading was delivered in London in February 1859 by Brookfield himself, and the idea seems to have been taken up enthusiastically, for Plumptre later reported that around 50 public reading circles had come into existence in England and Wales, some being so popular that listeners had to be turned away. Most of these circles were organized through the London Public Reading Society, although some existed independently. Many of these circles, however, struggled to obtain good leaders and, like the National Home Reading Union circles which followed them, had a precarious existence because of their voluntary nature.[5]

The model upon which the National Home Reading Union organized its reading circles was the Chautauqua Reading Circle[6] in America, described by Fitch in the *Nineteenth century* in 1888.[7] This reading circle originated in the Chautauqua Assembly, which began as a camp meeting of the Methodist Episcopal Church in 1871. The first readings were based upon the Bible, but secular readings were gradually added, one of which was a Teachers' Reading Union which extended the annual retreat into a home reading circle to continue the promotion of reading and study throughout the year. This Union, according to Fitch, 'suggests the names of suitable books, facilitates the circulation of them among the readers, and provides three regular and several advanced courses of professional reading, supplementing the book work by written correspondence and records of experience, and by special counsels forwarded by the professor to registered members'. By 1878, this circle had developed into a Literary and Scientific Reading Circle, with a membership of approximately 100,000 throughout the United States. Fitch believed that a similar scheme would be feasible in Britain, where, he thought, the rapidly expanding reading population needed to be protected from the dangers of desultory and aimless reading and the influences of bad books, and where there would be many 'persons of leisure and scholarly tastes, who would rejoice to render service, if only the way were made clear to them and definite direction were issued for guidance'. Paton, intrigued by Fitch's account of the Chautauqua scheme, and almost certainly aware that the universities of Oxford and Cambridge had just launched a scheme for the promotion of home reading though the University Extension Scheme,[8] was quickly convinced that a similar project was needed in Britain, and consequently formed the National Home Reading Union in April 1889.[9] The inaugural meeting took place at the Earl of Aberdeen's residence, and was attended by several leading figures from the worlds of literature, education and the Church. A number of prominent personages, among them the Archbishop of Canterbury, Robert Browning, and the Duke of Argyll, consented to be vice-presidents of the Union. The event was noticed by *The Times*,[10] which recorded that: 'The scheme proposes to draw up courses of reading for different classes of readers, especially for young people and artisans, which will be so planned as to interest the mind as well as convey useful information'; these objectives were to be achieved through the establishment of local reading and discussion circles, the publication of a magazine and the organization of summer assemblies at which lectures would be delivered.

Reading holidays

The summer assemblies were considered by the Union to be an effective means of publicity in its early days, although their importance in this respect faded after a few years. In Paton's words, the rationale for the summer assemblies was that 'lectures and excursions instruct; conferences inspire; social intercourse encourages members to remain in loyal union with the society';[11] they would also contribute to the rational recreation ideal by bringing differing social classes into contact. The first summer school was held at Blackpool in 1889, a symbolic venue chosen for its emphasis upon the type of indulgent amusement that Paton was anxious to displace, and because its holiday season concentration of artisans, Paton's 'hard-headed folk of the northern manufacturing districts', was precisely the type of membership the Union hoped to recruit.[12] John Churton Collins, one of the Union's most prominent supporters, depicted the Blackpool assembly in colourful terms:

> Within a few hours one of the gayest and idlest of watering-places found itself transformed, as if by magic, into a University. Bewildered visitors and inhabitants gazed in wonder at theatres and concert-halls placarded with names which they had never seen anywhere but on the title pages of books and in the columns of literary and scientific reviews.

At the end of the fortnight, the future success of the National Home Reading Union in bringing moral and intellectual recreation to thousands of people seemed assured to Churton Collins,[13] but, although he was able to claim that some lectures were attended by more than 500 people, the absence of any reference to their degree of success in attracting the working classes for whom they were largely intended suggests that they failed in this aim. In 1891, a third summer assembly, again held at Blackpool, included lectures on

'Chemistry for boys and girls', 'Five great English statesmen' and 'English Literature of the Eighteenth Century', this last being delivered by Churton Collins himself.[14] Later, summer assemblies moved away from commercial seaside resorts to fashionable inland spas and towns, and quickly developed into middle-class holidays, typified by the 1903 assembly in Ross on Wye, held in one of the town's premier hotels.[15] The Union appears to have been somewhat optimistic if not indeed naive in its belief that the assemblies would appeal to working-class holiday-makers; as Alex Hill, later a president of the Union commented, the vision of mill hands and ironworkers devoting their annual holiday to the pursuit of intellectual exercise was 'begotten in the ecstasy of the contemplation of the world as it may be when the Union has recreated it. In the meantime it is a different class which alone is willing to spend its holiday in seeking mental stimulus, and this class demands a different local setting for its summer school'.[16]

READING CIRCLES

Important as the assemblies were to the maintenance of a national network for the Union, the main element of the Union's work was the establishment of local reading circles. A National Home Reading Union circle had a minimum of five members, and met under the guidance of a leader who provided the link between the circle and the head office. At the start of a session, the Union published lists of books to be studied, from which each circle could select those it wished to study. Three such lists were prepared: Young Peoples', Artisans' and General Readers'. However, by 1903, the Artisans' lists had been replaced by Special lists, again suggesting a failure to appeal to working-class readers. Circles met on a fortnightly or monthly basis to discuss the chosen books, either by responding to formal papers read by the leader or by members themselves, or by discussing them informally. The Union provided support to local circles by establishing a network through which circles could borrow books from other circles and by preparing portfolios of illustrative prints and photographs to accompany the listed books. It also published three magazines, one to support each of the lists, which provided information about and suggested discussion topics for the recommended books and general news about the Union. Many magazine articles concluded with questions, and members were encouraged to submit answers to the editor, who read and commented upon them and then returned them to the reader. The Union enjoyed a good measure of initial success in recruitment; 7,714 members had been enrolled by 1893,[17] while in 1896 alone over 8,000 new members were recruited.[18] *The Times* commented that it seemed '. . . to be doing useful work in promoting systematic reading, recreative and instructive, among young and old, as a means of continued education',[19] and noted again in 1897 that:

> So much reading is desultory and ineffective for want of guidance that the direction and information gained by joining such a society as this ought to be useful to many who would like to do some definite reading if only they knew where to begin. One idea of the Union is to form local circles for mutual help and interest in systematic reading under the guidance, if possible, of some qualified leader.[20]

By 1909, the membership of the Union was approximately 8,000, of whom 5,000 were members of a reading circle, and there were a further 6,000 associated members through the provision of the Introductory Course in the magazine of the Co-operative Holidays Association. The Union forged links with schools, particularly in London, and claimed that 40,000 children were associated through school membership;[21] Union offices were also established in Australia and South Africa.

Activities at a local level

Information about National Home Reading Union reading circles is difficult to trace, as the localized nature of the circles has resulted in geographically scattered records. However, to judge from available local records and from information published centrally by the Union, it seems that most circles were relatively small in size and were predominantly middle-class in composition. For example, the first reunion of the five Southport circles, which was held in Rowntree's cafe in 1905, consisted of speeches by the town's literati, glees, songs, recitals and games,[22] and seems unlikely to have attracted a substantial working-class attendance.

Many circles were connected with Congregational churches, and thus embodied Paton's vision of a practised Christianity; indeed, the Congregational ideal of a missionary outlook and a civic gospel is evident in much of the Union's literature. The following quotation from the Union's magazine, which prompts the comparison of the promotion of reading to evangelism is typical of its style: 'The missionary outlook which thinks of sharing intellectual pleasures and rousing love of books where none exists is the very salt of the Union and, if the new session is to be a worthy and successful one, it must be made so by our members themselves and their enthusiasm'.[23]

The Christ Church reading circle at Goole was based on the Congregational chapel of that name and had a membership of 24 in 1904.[24] At Hull, there was a circle in connection with the Albion Congregational Church Young People's Association; this had ten members who met in each other's homes on Saturday evenings, thus suggesting that reading circles were important for social as well as educational reasons. Even in remoter rural areas, the existence of a flourishing Congregational church offered a context in which a National Home Reading Union circle could quickly become established; the tiny hamlet of Knowle Green in the Ribble Valley, for example, boasted a circle of 27 members as early as 1890.[25] Further evidence of the strong links between the Union and the Congregational church is the fact that Union New Year Reunions were frequently held in Congregational schools.[26] Many circles flourished outside the Congregationalist environment, and combined informal education with social events and entertainment. The Edinburgh circle met monthly at the house of a member and read and discussed until 9.30pm, when 'simple refreshments are served and conversation becomes general', and also organized social evenings in winter and excursions in summer;[27] another circle was described by a member as a valuable addition to the town`s social life.[28] While the Union was doubtless pleased with the spread of reading circles, it remained concerned that they should be essentially forums for the discussion of literature and reminded members through its magazine that: ' . . . a Circle is meant to be an organised body of Readers, all taking the same Course or Courses, and meeting together at stated intervals under the Presidency of a Leader. A number of members doing all sorts of work according to the individual fancy of each is not a Circle'.[29]

The works prescribed by the Union varied, depending on the list in which they were published. The first list in the Artisan's Section, issued in 1889, included Carlyle's *Past and present*, Dickens' *A tale of two cities* and a number of biographies of working men,[30] while the Special course which replaced this comprised subjects such as modern French social philosophy, the novels and poetry of George Meredith and Cervantes and other Spanish writers. The General Readers' list in 1905 typifies the more readily accessible nature of this section, and included Jefferies' *The open air*, Social Movements as reflected in Mrs Gaskell's *Mary Barton* and Landmarks of European History.

THE NATIONAL HOME READING UNION AND PUBLIC LIBRARIES

There was a close affinity between the objectives of the Union and those of public libraries. As one observer commented in the *Nineteenth century*:

> The librarian has to be very careful not only what he recommends, but how he suggests the advantages of reading any particular books . . . May I ask the librarians who are taking charge of our growing Free Libraries to occasionally invite the working classes to their libraries, say a few words to them about books, show them some good specimens . . .[31]

Because of the similarity between the objectives of the National Home

Reading Union and those of librarians interested in guidance and systematic reading, it seems inevitable, with the benefit of hindsight, that some form of collaboration should have evolved. Librarians and library committees were enthusiastic about the aims of the Union almost from its inception; as early as 1892, the Fleetwood Public Library Committee authorized the display of a Union card in the library's reading room.[32] Even where no formal collaboration developed, the Union had a marked influence on public library practice, for many libraries organized reading circles based upon the Union's model.

Two events in particular contributed to the development of a partnership between the Union and public libraries. The first of these occurred through the University Extension Movement, with which, ironically, Paton had been reluctant for the Union to be closely involved because of its lack of a national base.[33] In 1900, John Passmore Edwards, a noted benefactor of public libraries in the south of England, sponsored a series of library lectures in London under the auspices of the London Society for the Extension of University Training. These lectures were held in public libraries with librarians acting as secretaries and each lecture being followed by a discussion of the books read. Attendances were encouragingly high: 310 at Brixton, 230 at Fulham and 240 at Battersea. They attracted the notice of the *Daily News*, which commented not only upon their proof of the need for direction in reading, but which observed also that they suggested exciting possibilities for Free Libraries.[34] The second factor was the programme of University Extension classes provided at Toynbee Hall, which attracted approximately 1,000 visitors each week. Charles Booth[35] noticed these lectures, and commented on the ways in which lecturers were brought into contact with students not only through formal classes but also through social and extra-mural events, one of which was the Toynbee Library Readers' Union, formed in 1891 to bring readers together for the purposes of literary and social discussion. The librarian of this Readers' Union, C. F. Newcombe, felt that a similar type of project might do much to address the problems then being experienced by public libraries in their provision of fiction, and published his views in the *Library Association record*:[36]

> Could not this experiment be adopted more widely in public libraries in large towns? The formation of Library Readers' Unions would, I think, enormously help the work of a public library, and increase its power as a great centre of culture and education . . . [the fiction reader might return] . . . to the noble conceptions of duty embodied in the novels of George Eliot, to the wise and tender humanity of Dickens, the refreshed humour of Thackeray, and the sweet healthiness of Mrs. Gaskell's fiction.

The National Home Reading Union and public libraries each had much to gain through cooperation. Both had a mission to improve popular reading and to promote systematic reading, and libraries would have a new opportunity to progress from the impasse of the fiction question, while the Union would gain access to a potentially huge membership. There was the additional advantage that libraries could facilitate access to the recommended books. Despite the apparent benefits of collaboration, formal institutional cooperation was slow to develop and little progress was made until 1903, when Alex Hill, chairman of the Union, addressed the Library Association conference[37] to outline the practical steps public libraries could take towards cooperative work, which were:

- enrol public librarians as honorary members of the Union
- display Union cards in public libraries
- encourage and facilitate the formation of public library-based NHRU circles
- make library rooms available for Union circle meetings
- stock titles recommended by the Union.

Hill repeated his appeal in the *Library*, in a revealingly titled article 'Responsibility for the public taste',[38] the paternalistic tone of which starkly exposed the rational recreational idealism and cultural superiority which underpinned the work of the Union. Some insight to the Union's ideology can be gained by quoting from the article:

> Is the public the best judge of what is good for its moral and intellectual health? To credit the public with a power of discriminating between what is wholesome and what is harmful is to admit that it possesses literary knowledge of which it is pathetically destitute . . . The average man from whom the business of life extracts a daily tale of eight hours' work enters a library with no idea of the subject which is likely to interest him . . . no librarian, no library committee need feel hesitation in guiding the reading of the great majority of their clients.

At a local level, many librarians supported the aims of the National Home Reading Union, and The Library Association gave official affirmation of collaborative work in 1904.[39] Despite such institutional approval, cooperative ventures were slow to start and were also vulnerable once in operation because of they depended solely upon voluntary effort. To encourage progress, the Union eventually undertook to find leaders for library-based circles and to allow libraries to incorporate a Union magazine, the *Readers' Review*, in local library magazines. In 1908, Paton himself issued a further appeal to librarians,[40] describing libraries as the 'mission halls of culture', but despite frequent formal statements of support for cooperation, relationships between libraries and the Union were never totally harmonious because librarians feared that the Union would, so to speak, steal their thunder. Librarians also disliked the patronizing tone of the Union's communiqués, many of which conveyed the impression that public libraries themselves needed advice in selecting their books, and there was also much concern about the extra workload involved in the organization of a reading circle. Nevertheless, some libraries did organize Union circles, although one observer estimated that in 1911 only 105 out of approximately 600 libraries were honorary members of the Union, and that of these only five organized circles in direct connection with the Union.[41]

Much of what little documentary evidence of reading circles exists was written by their organizers and tends to be subjective. Personal reminiscences of members of circles, such as the following extract, are rarer still, but provide some insight to the nature of a Union reading circle:

> One circle I remember met in a room of a public library to discuss Hobson's 'Problems of poverty'; we were a strangely incongruous gathering of men and women – Tories, Fabians, members of the I.L.P., who rubbed each other's angles down and gained, I hope, in toleration and sympathy.
>
> Another evening circle which met fortnightly for many years in the houses of various members, was more in the nature of a social gathering.[42]

Reading circles doubtlessly varied in form and structure between localities, and would reflect the chosen style of the leader. While circles organized in members' houses could incorporate social objectives, perhaps even with these as their major purpose, circles based in public libraries were obliged to emphasize their literary interests. Many libraries organized circles based on the National Home Reading Union model without joining the Union; such was the case at Bromley where reading circles met each Tuesday at 8.00pm to discuss the works of a particular writer. Harris, the librarian, reported[43] a typical evening's programme as follows:

8.00 Start.
8.05 Short biographical sketch of the chosen author.
8.20 Each member to read a prepared poem from any source or from the author chosen for the evening. Each reading not to last more than ten minutes. Questions and answers expected after each reading.
9.30 Short critical essay by a member to last not more than ten minutes to be followed by a short discussion.
9.50 Closing poem from any source.

The writers studied on this particular course included Tennyson, Keats, Goldsmith, Browning, Shelley and Byron. Unfortunately, there is no description of the membership of the circle.

Reading circles tended to be durable; at the time of Harris' writing, the Bromley circle had been in existence for seven years. Few circles, however, established a mass appeal; that at Darwen library had fewer than 50 members,[44] while the library based circle at Colne had 20.[45]

The Stepney Public Library Reading Circle

The first National Home Reading Union circle to be established in conjunction with a public library was in Stepney in the winter of 1903, primarily through the enthusiasm of Cawthorne, the librarian. The stated objective of the Stepney circle was to 'encourage systematic reading and profitable use of the libraries by drawing attention to the best authors and suggesting and providing interesting courses of reading'.[46] National Home Reading Union reading circles were established in five Stepney libraries, some of which were located in the poorest parts of London. Initial attendances were encouraging: 32 at the Limehouse course on Ruskin and 24 at the Whitechapel course on English literature 1688–1879. Membership rapidly fell, however, and the circles were eventually merged in 1907 into a Stepney Readers' Union, which held 24 meetings in 1907–8 under the librarian's chairmanship, with an average attendance of 32. Like other circles, the Stepney Union depended upon voluntary effort and, although the secretary worked assiduously, there were frequent difficulties in obtaining the services of guest lecturers. The Union was further hampered when, in 1910, the Local Government Board Auditor ruled that lecturers' fees could not be paid through the library rate, thus causing the library staff more work in raising funds through subscription[47] and eventually the demise of the Union.

THE DECLINE OF THE NATIONAL HOME READING UNION

Although Paton was not greatly involved in the management of the Union after the turn of the century, his death in 1911 deprived the Union of its figurehead and source of inspiration. The First World War further weakened the Union, for although it continued to operate, it proved difficult to maintain circle memberships, which in some instances fell to as little as two or three.[48] After the war, the Union began to experience financial difficulties, many of which were brought about by the costs of publishing and distributing its magazine, and was forced to raise subscription fees and the price of the magazine on a number of occasions; by 1921, the fees had risen to three shillings and sixpence for the General Course and two shillings and sixpence for the Young People's Course. Nevertheless, the magazines published in the early 1920s contain several reports of flourishing circles, many of which were now organized by, or included large proportions of, schoolteachers. However, by 1925, the financial situation had deteriorated further, and in order to raise extra funds the Union's magazine was redesigned as *The reader*, a more general literary magazine, and became available on general sale. This was not, however, an ultimately successful undertaking, and in 1930 the National Home Reading Union became financially non-viable and ceased to exist.

The social, technological and cultural changes which occurred between the end of the nineteenth century and the middle of the inter-war period meant that the National Home Reading Union finally had no role. Public libraries had spread, largely into rural and remote areas, as a result of the Public Libraries Act of 1919, and many urban libraries had begun to organize wireless lectures and related discussion groups. Literature itself was losing its primary cultural status as the English novel gradually ceased to be a medium for the conveyance of dominant cultural values, while radio and the cinema were becoming increasingly important as mediums of mass communication. Nevertheless, the National Home Reading Union had a record in which it could take some pride. Although it never established a firm base among working-class readers, it did manage to operate, almost entirely on voluntary labour, for several decades. As the final issue of *The reader* commented:

> The N.H.R.U. has published a magazine for forty years, its latest form, *The Reader*, having run for five years. This is, we feel, not a bad record in these days when every year new magazines rise and fail. The early magazine supplied guidance to readers at a time when there were no B.B.C. lectures, W.E.A., and other classes, or improved public library services such as there are now. *The Reader*, changing its form in accord with modern needs and conditions, has tried to introduce readers, in its courses and booklists, to many different subjects of study. If it has stimulated curiosity it will have achieved something.[49]

NOTES AND REFERENCES TO CHAPTER 8

Abbreviations
NHRU – National Home Reading Union

1   Paton, J. L., *John Brown Paton: a biography*, Hodder and Stoughton, 1914, 212–3.
2   Paton, op. cit., 219.
3   Besant, W., *All sorts and conditions of men*, Chatto and Windus, 1903

(originally published in 1882). Besant expounded his idea of a Palace of the People which would provide study and intellectual effort as a form of recreation for those who worked in 'uncongenial and tedious labour' in his article 'The amusements of the people', published in *Contemporary review*, March 1884, 342–53.

4   Plumptre, C. J., 'On the formation of public reading societies as a recreation for the working classes', *Transactions of the National Association for the Promotion of Social Science*, 1861.

5   ibid.

6   The word Chautauqua is used by Robert Pirsig in *Zen and the art of motorcycle maintenance* (Bodley Head, 1974) to describe dialectic discussion; Pirsig identifies the origins of the phrase to those 'travelling tent-show Chautauquas . . . an old-time series of popular talks intended to edify and entertain, improve the mind and bring culture and enlightenment to the ears an thoughts of the hearer'.

7   Fitch, J. G., 'The Chautauqua reading circle', *Nineteenth century*, 24 October 1888, 487–500.

8   *The Times*, 28 November 1888.

9   Paton, op. cit., ref. 1, Chapter 16.

10   *The Times*, 16 April 1889.

11   Quoted in: Marchant, J., *J.B. Paton. M.A., D.D.: educational and social pioneer*, James Clarke, 1909, 253.

12   Paton, op. cit., 278–9.

13   Collins, J. C., 'The National Home Reading Union and its prospects', *Contemporary review*, 58, August 1890, 193–211.

14   *The Times*, 7 May 1891.

15   *NHRU magazine*, **15** (1), 7 October 1903.

16   Quoted in: Marchant, op. cit., ref. 11.

17   *The Times*, 20 November 1894.

18   *The Times*, 1 February 1897.

19   *The Times*, 25 October 1895.

20   *The Times*, 3 September 1897.

21   Marchant, op. cit., ref. 11, 258.

22   *NHRU magazine (General Course)*, **16** (5), 7 February 1905.

23   *NHRU magazine*, **15** (1), October 1903.

24   *NHRU magazine (General Course)*, **14** (4), 7 December 1905.

25   *Lancashire Congregational Calendar 1890*.

26   *NHRU magazine (General Course)*, **17** (4), 7 December 1905.

27   Correspondence in *NHRU magazine*, **15** (3) 54.

28   *NHRU magazine (General Course)*, **15** (9) 211.

29   *NHRU monthly journal. Artisan's Section*, **3**, December 1889.

30   *NHRU monthly journal. Artisan's Section*, 1 October 1889.
31   Humphrey, G. R., 'The reading of the working classes', *Nineteenth century*, **3**, 1893, 690–701.
32   *Fleetwood Public Libraries Act Minute Book*, 13 January 1892.
33   Paton, op. cit., ref. 1, 273.
34   *Daily News*, 15 December 1900.
35   Fried, A. and Elman, R. (eds.), *Charles Booths' London*, Hutchinson, 1969.
36   Newcombe, C. F., 'On Library Readers' Unions: their value and possibilities', *Library Association record*, December 1900, 623–9.
37   Hill, A., 'Public libraries and the National Home Reading Union', *Library Association record*, 1903, 615–22.
38   Hill, A., Responsibility for the public taste', *Library*, July 1906, 257–62.
39   *Preliminary report of the Committee on Public Education and Public Libraries to the Newcastle meeting of The Library Association*, 1904.
40   Paton, J. B., 'Public libraries and the National Home Reading Union', *Library Association record*, 1908, 488–97.
41   Pomfret, J., 'Reading circles', *Library world*, 1911, 289–94.
42   *NHRU magazine*, **30** (2), November 1918.
43   Harris, W. J., 'The organisation and conduct of reading circles; adult and junior', *Library world*, **17**, 1914–15, 69–72.
44   Pomfret, J., 'Reading circles', *Library world*, 1911, 289–94.
45   *NHRU magazine (General Course)*, **16** (7), 7 April 1905, 170.
46   Borough of Stepney, *Public Libraries Committee Report*, 1904.
47   Stepney Public Library, *Annual Report 1911–12*.
48   *Home reading magazine*, May 1920.
49   *The reader*, **5** (12), 1930.

Chapter 9
Fiction, Library Committees and Ideology

INTRODUCTION

Public libraries dealt with the provision of novels and recreational literature in varying ways. The patterns of treatment were marked out on the one side by a literary hierarchy with its distinctions between 'high' literary and 'low' popular fiction, and on the other by an emerging liberal acceptance of popular fiction as a form of undemanding escapist relaxation and a willingness to provide popular fiction to produce a high rate of library use. A third feature was the smaller but still influential call either to ban fiction altogether or at least to charge for its borrowing. This chapter discusses the extent to which the practices outlined in the case studies might provide a more generalized insight to public library development and its social context between 1850 and the First World War.

FICTION PROVISION AND URBAN POWER STRUCTURES

The major issue to emerge from the ways in which libraries handled the Great Fiction Question concerns the role of the library committee. In any library authority, the treatment of fiction and indeed the development of the whole library service was ultimately determined by the library committee and not by the librarian. Librarians undoubtedly influenced committee members and advised them on the latest technical developments in library practice, not least through the fact that it was normal for the chairman of the committee to accompany the librarian to the Library Association's annual conferences at which the latest developments and issues were discussed, and in a small number of authorities librarians were entrusted with some measure of responsibility in the book selection process. However, it was the elected members and not the professional employee who had the final say both in strategic planning and in many of the week-to-week operational matters too. A library committee was not simply a random collection of individuals, but a body which represented economic, political, religious and social forces.

Eminent historians[1] have shown us that events generally have a multiplicity of causes, and it would be unwise to attribute the treatment of fiction in any particular library solely to the committee as there would have been several other influential factors: among them, the nature of donations of books received, pressure from the library profession, the activities of local interest groups such as the National Home Reading Union, and not least the extent of the demand for popular fiction. However, knowledge of library development at a local level suggests that, in terms of the provision of fiction in public libraries, the economic, social, political and religious composition of the library committee was a major factor of influence.

In being under the close control of their committees, public libraries were no different to other local government services, and thus the whole issue of the composition and influence of library committees becomes significant in the context of urban local government of the period. In his study of Rochdale, Bolton and Salford, Garrard[2] showed that considerable municipal power was exercised by councillors and committee members, and that the persons who held council office were in the main drawn from a social and economic elite. It is worth mentioning that council meetings were frequently held at four o'clock in the afternoon, thereby making it extremely difficult – if not impossible – for working-class people to participate in municipal affairs. Not only were town councils usually dominated by those who held positions of power in other spheres, but it was normal for committees in all departments to take a much closer active interest in the operational details of the service provided than is the case nowadays. Hennock[3] describes how councillors would visit condemned houses, or check the bookkeeping in the treasurer's department, and the selection of books for the library would naturally appear to be a task of sufficient importance to be undertaken by council members, particularly as it involved both the expenditure of public money and the maintenance of an image of respectability in the bookstock. The following quotation is taken from a report by John Ballinger following an investigation of library committees in 1895, and illustrates the extent, in this instance in Belfast, of councillors' active involvement and the limited scope of many librarians:

> The Library Committee shall manage the Free Library and the Museum in connection therewith, shall receive and arrange and take all necessary proceedings with respect to any articles included in any presentation, donation, gift or bequest to the Corporation for the Library or Museum. They shall examine and pay, or certify for payment, all accounts relating to matters within the province of the committee.[4]

Library committees and fiction provision

Given the extent of committee control, the provision of fiction in any town library should, in the first instance, be evaluated with reference to the committee. In Darwen, where, as we have seen, the committee viewed the library service as a means of implementing a civic gospel, the encouragement of uplifting reading and the accompanying censorship of non-improving popular leisure in the form of popular romances and tales took the form of a missionary crusade. The ideal of rational recreation was much in evidence, as the committee's efforts to change patterns of recreational reading were directed mainly towards working-class readers, and the initiatives undertaken in cooperation with the National Home Reading Union were, at least nominally, intended to bring the middle and working classes closer together through a leisure experience. Although the Darwen committee was predominantly Liberal, the religious element of Congregationalism was of greater significance in determining the character of the library service, because the origins of the civic gospel were based in this;[5] it is worth noting in this context that not all Liberal councils espoused the civic gospel. There was an evident desire to exercise a form of cultural censorship over what was borrowed and read, and although neither the restrictions on the purchase of popular fiction nor the organization of National Home Reading Union circles were tremendously successful in the long term, the intention to achieve some degree of control was nevertheless present.

In Blackburn, the library committee adopted a markedly different approach by providing the non-literary popular novels for which there was an expressed public demand, by interpreting issues inflated by fiction as an indicator of success and by displaying a disinterested attitude to literary fiction. Here, the dominant presence of large-scale industrial employers and Conservatives on the library committee appears to have been more important than the accompanying Anglicanism, because the paternalist rationale for fiction provision was of an economic and political rather than of a religious nature. It is interesting to note that the pragmatism of the Blackburn library committee is still a common feature of Conservative-dominated library committees, as Bob Usherwood has recently shown.[6] In Wigan, the library committee's laissez-faire attitude to fiction resulted in provision through default, and was also paternalistic in nature, though in a rather more passive form than was the case in Blackburn. Again, the committee's political characteristics were more influential than the religious, but the influence of the chairman of the committee and that of the long-serving librarian were also important factors. The establishment in Wigan of a subscription scheme owed more to pragmatism and economic circumstances than to ideological conviction, though it is again interesting that recent research has suggested that there is currently more support for the concept of a premium service among Conservative members of library committees than amongst those of other political parties.[7]

There are differing interpretations of paternalism, just as there were differing forms of paternalistic practice. The idea of paternalism is most closely associated with employers such as Robert Owen, Titus Salt, and the Greg Brothers, who believed they had a moral duty to demonstrate a concerned interest in the welfare of their workpeople by providing housing, education, open spaces, gardens and other services and amenities. Such paternalism was by no means restricted to Conservative-Anglican employers, as the names mentioned above readily show. However, the essential feature of all paternalism was that it was essentially self-interested, being based upon a recognition of the economic and social benefits of maintaining a healthy, stable and reliable workforce. In the second half of the nineteenth century, the paternalism which had originated in benevolent individual employers became increasingly a characteristic feature of municipal government as manufacturers and businessmen were elected or coopted to councils and committees. Individual philanthropy continued to flourish, but was gradually overshadowed by the sheer economy of scale of municipal provision – one public park or one public library reaching several times the number of people as one private garden or one factory reading room. This collective paternalism was manifest in a wide range of services and facilities which improved the conditions of urban life, among which public libraries were but one form, and as Patrick Joyce says:

> The new paternalism was to coincide with the growth of civic Britain. Public libraries and parks, public health and the building of town halls were all causes to which employers and merchants contributed liberally in terms of land, money and time. Public utilities, such as gas and water supply, were also developed under the aegis of those whose consumer interest was greatest, the employers of labour.[8]

The mill owners and factory employers who occupied the positions of power on urban councils were drawn from an industrial milieu in which recreational provision in the form of factory clubs, works teams, excursions, dinners and libraries was widely promoted, and they naturally understood the economic and social benefits of a corresponding range of municipal amenities. The provision of a public library service which supplied working-class readers, many of whom would work for or have some family-based economic dependence upon the employers who formed the council, with popular fiction was thus one means by which employers could, through municipal provision, continue paternalist practice in a different context and on a wider scale.

Generalization

What seemed initially to be simple questions of whether or not to provide novels, or what types of novels to supply, were in fact extremely complex because they brought into focus many conflicting values, beliefs and political and religious opinions, and because public library approaches to fiction provision differed so much from one town to another. The Victorian town was indeed, as Mark Girouard[9] says, a battlefield: Conservatives fought Liberals, brewers fought temperance reformers, religious groups fought immorality, literary societies set themselves against popular fiction, and the middle classes sought to reform the uncouth recreational pastimes of the working classes. The feasibility of extracting from this diverse practice anything which could be useful in developing a more general understanding of fiction provision in public libraries and, by extension, of the origins of local authority leisure provision, seems initially questionable. The value of any historical study of leisure and libraries would be diminished, however, if an interpretative approach were to be abandoned for a narrative, and it is worth exploring the extent to which the historical development of fiction provision might illuminate the evolution of the social role of the library.

First of all, it is worth considering what sort of generalization would be valid and useful. The most alluring generalization, that Liberal–Congregationalist committees and Conservative–Anglican committees always developed library services comparable to those described in earlier chapters, is not, unfortunately, tenable. The Conservatives on Warrington's library committee, for example, where the subscription library was maintained for many years at a direct disadvantage to working-class fiction readers, were hardly acting in a benevolent paternalist fashion when compared to Blackburn.

A more rewarding strategy would be to consider the influence of library committees upon library practice not in terms of an historical or narrative event based upon time, place and sequence, but as a sociological process based upon functional relationships. The benefit of this would lie not in the development of an historical model of library practice with a universal applicability, but in the recognition and explanation of the processes of change which determined library practice in geographical and historical terms. History and sociology complement each other in this process, and, as the noted library historian, Thomas Kelly, has said, library history is more revealing if it incorporates a sociological dimension.[10] The library committees described in this book were composed of relatively homogeneous socio-economic and religious groups. Becoming a member of a library committee was in itself what Abrams[11] refers to as a socially structured process; in other words, committee members were not individuals who lived and worked outside the social structures of their time, but were a part of them. The members of library committees represented political, economic and religious values and beliefs and their actions were in effect a realization of these values and beliefs. The councillors and committee men who dominated local government in the period before the First World War constituted a power elite in terms of urban politics, but they were also members of other urban elites – economic, religious and social; indeed, at the turn of the century the structure of political municipal power in urban areas commonly corresponded almost exactly to the social structure.[12] Members tended to be drawn from the higher socio-economic groups, and the characteristics of respectability, social rank, property, wealth and education which had been considered the crucial attributes of town councillors in the middle of the nineteenth century were still widely regarded in the period covered by this book. A municipal replication of socio-economic influence and status was characteristic of all the library committees encountered in the preceding chapters, which were composed of large-scale industrial employers such as cotton manufacturers and colliery owners, landed gentry and professional men. Even where working-class representation existed, it was, as Hennock notes, one thing to participate and another to dominate.[13]

Libraries and the dominant ideology

Through varying approaches to the selection of fiction and the promotion of recreational reading, library committees controlled fiction provision in a way which they perceived would promote their own values and interests – economic, political, religious, cultural, or a mixture of these. Public libraries were thus instrumental, in a perhaps minor but important way, in supporting the power structure of their local community. They were not neutral, as conventional library history would sometimes suggest, but were expressions of political and religious beliefs, of cultural and literary values, and of both restrictive and relaxed attitudes to popular leisure. To state this is not to underestimate the undoubted educational and social benefits that libraries brought to thousands of readers, but simply to acknowledge the difficulties in a public institution concerned with communications, ideas and beliefs remaining independent or free from external influence. The frequently expressed maxim that politics should be kept out of libraries, and vice versa, could not be realized as long as libraries lay within the politician's sphere of influence. Libraries existed within society, not beyond it, and were subject, like all other public institutions, to what was culturally normal and socially acceptable. They were also provided through public money, and were controlled by politicians at a local, and ultimately at a national, level. It is rewarding to consider to what degree public library fiction provision might be argued to have been shaped by what Althusser[14] called the 'Cultural Ideological State Apparatus' – the means by which culture, including literature and fiction, may be manipulated or controlled to support a dominant ideology principally through persuasive means, but in which censorship or repression also plays a part. With reference to libraries, this would include the promotion of novels which conveyed dominant moral and cultural values, but, in a secondary and more tacit way, the censorship or even the simple non-selection of fiction was a means of repressing the expression of alternative cultural values and political beliefs. This pattern of practice was most clearly evident in Darwen library's treatment of fiction which was described earlier, but the general debate of the fiction question also reveals many elements of a wish to influence or control what people read for leisure. Elements of this type of practice extended far beyond the provision of fiction; for example, many public libraries would not take socialist publications, and, as we have seen, betting news was blacked from the newspapers in an attempt to stop working men participating in off-course betting. The Conservative-controlled Blackburn library committee refused for many years in the late nineteenth and early twentieth centuries to provide socialist newspapers in its reading room, despite repeated requests from working-class organizations, even though it reacted positively to the working-class demand for popular fiction, which, unlike the newspaper, brought no political benefits to the library's users. In terms of the individual library authority of the nineteenth century, Althusser's proposition seems to be meaningful largely in terms of a localized ideology, but it is interesting to note that there are indications of its relevance in more recent, albeit slightly different, contexts. Perhaps the most prominent example lies in the refusals to stock radical and alternative newspapers throughout the 1970s and 1980s, which occurred despite codes of conduct and policies proclaiming neutrality and impartiality. The Adam Smith Institute's *Ex libris*[15] criticized political influence upon public libraries from trade unions and left-wing groups, but failed to remark upon the more widespread practice of simply declining to select publications from socialist radical and non-party political groups.[16] As Usherwood has shown, issues concerning stock selection in libraries are still actively discussed by public library committees, and political ideology inevitably influences the attitudes and opinions of many individual committee members.[17] Further analytical studies of public library development are now needed to provide a more complete picture of the library's structural role, but the evidence available to date does indicate that, in the period covered by this book, the selection of fiction offered opportunities for the implementation of the dominant beliefs and values of a community's power elite.

NOTES AND REFERENCES TO CHAPTER 9

1   For example: Elton, G. R., *Political history: principles and practice*, Allen Lane, 1970; Carr, E., *What is history*, Macmillan, 1961.
2   Garrard, J., *Leadership and power in Victorian industrial towns 1830–80*, Manchester University Press, 1983.
3   Hennock, E. P., *Fit and proper persons: ideal and reality in nineteenth century urban government*, Arnold, 1973.
4   Ballinger, J., Report on the constitution of library committees, *Library*, 7, 1895, 1–8.
5   The cultural dimension of the civic gospel and its significance to public library development is discussed briefly in Richards, J., 'The cinema and cinema-going in Birmingham in the 1930s', in Walton, J. and Walvin, J. (eds.), *Leisure in Britain 1780–1939*, Manchester University Press, 1983, 31–52.
6   Usherwood, R. C., *Public library politics: the role of the elected member*, Library Association Publishing, 1993, passim.
7   Usherwood, op. cit., ref. 6, 179–82.
8   Joyce, P., *Work, society and politics: the culture of the factory in later Victorian England*, Methuen, 1980, 169.
9   Girouard, M., *The English town*, Yale University Press, 1990, 190.
10   Kelly, T., 'Thoughts on the writing of library history', *Library history*, 3, 1975, 161–9.
11   Abrams, P., *Historical sociology*, Open Books, 1982, 280.
12   Birch, A. H., *Small town politics, A study of political life in Glossop*, Oxford University Press, 1959.
13   Hennock, op. cit., ref. 3, 308–34.
14   Althusser, L., 'Ideology and Ideological state apparatuses', in *Lenin and philosophy and other essays*, New Left Books, 1971, 121–73.
15   *Ex libris*, Adam Smith Institute, 1986.
16   See: Snape, R. J., *Radical readers and public libraries: a cultural study*, Public Libraries Research Group, 1986.
17   Usherwood, op. cit., ref. 6, 67–74.

Chapter 10
Endnote

PUBLIC LIBRARIES AND LEISURE – THE FUTURE

The main aim of this book was to explain the historical treatment of public library fiction and to show how the public library acquired its role as a leisure provider. In conclusion, it would seem useful to assess the relevance of past experiences with fiction to the present and the immediate future. The Great Fiction Question may no longer be a central concern in librarianship, but the public library's leisure function and its role within public sector leisure provision has a reasonable claim to be one of the more pressing current issues. Despite the information revolution of the past two decades and its implications, public libraries seem certain to continue to be major leisure providers for the reasons described in the opening chapter, and their significance in this is likely to increase rather than diminish.

The focal period of this book concluded in 1914 – 80 years ago at the time of writing – and profound changes have occurred since then. There is no simplistic way in which current practice can be explained or future trends predicted by what happened before the First World War, but there seems nevertheless to be some merit in identifying connecting themes. The first of these concerns the purpose or rationale for providing leisure facilities and services through the public sector, which is as prominent an issue of debate currently as it was in the nineteenth century. There are differing and sometimes conflicting rationales for public sector leisure provision which have potentially differing impacts upon the library service.[1]

Rationales for public sector leisure

The first major public sector input to leisure provision emerged in the mid-nineteenth century when the government invested resources, directly and indirectly, in the control of disruptive forms of leisure and in the amelioration of the squalid urban conditions of the period. Permissive legislation enabled local authorities to develop services and facilities, such as public libraries, which directed or influenced aspects of peoples' lives and promoted social harmony. It is interesting to note that many services and facilities now universally recognized as core leisure provision were originally introduced for other reasons: baths for hygiene and parks for health, to give two examples. A major objective of this investment was to provide alternatives to drunkenness, depravity and other socially deviant forms of leisure.

The provision of public sector leisure to displace deviant forms of leisure is a recurring theme. Two examples from the more recent past are the expansion in provision for youth leisure in the 1960s which was largely motivated by a concern about juvenile delinquency, and the integrated leisure projects of the 1980s to contain mass unemployment and social unrest by investment in leisure.[2] Many such projects involved a wide range of institutions from the public, commercial and voluntary sectors, but rarely the public library.

From the 1880s onwards, the importance of leisure to the well-being of the individual gained a more general social acceptance and was recognized as a legitimate area of government interest. Throughout the first half of the twentieth century, this view was not seriously challenged, and in the decades following the Second World War many aspects of leisure provision were gradually incorporated in the portfolio of welfare services, the public sector providing a minimum level safety-net standard of leisure provision. Public libraries were fortunate in being one of the few institutions providing a leisure service to be made statutory under the Public Libraries Act 1964, which affirmed the validity of recreation as one of their functions.

In the later 1960s and throughout the 1970s public sector leisure enjoyed a period of expansion as access to leisure opportunity acquired a status akin to a right of citizenship. It is worth noting that it was only in this phase of leisure development that the word 'leisure' generally began to displace the older term 'recreation'. In recognition of the increasing amount of time available for leisure, the 1975 White Paper *Sport and recreation*[3] suggested that the provision of public sector leisure facilities was a part of the 'general fabric of the social services'. Public sector rationale progressed from the older notions of control and regulation to a more positive view of leisure as an indicator of the quality of life. The word 'leisure' acquired its current meaning as a wide-embracing term, and brought together, in the context of local government, a wide range of functions which contributed to the cultural, artistic and sporting life of the community. Disadvantage in access to leisure was addressed through the definition of certain groups as recreationally deprived and to the implementation of policies designed to ensure that no one was avoidably excluded from leisure opportunity – hence the numerous outreach programmes to disadvantaged minorities which were as much a part of the public library service as they were of other forms of public sector leisure.[4] In so far as the emergence of a more liberal approach to leisure involved libraries, it included an expansion in the provision of non-print media for leisure purposes – mainly recorded sound, a virtual elimination of the banning of fiction, the gradual disappearance of restricted fiction cupboards and the building of new libraries incorporating meeting and recital rooms. At its best, this period saw some efforts to bring libraries and leisure closer together, notably through the development of dual-use facilities, but local government structures and professional mistrust often militated against the success of many such ventures.

This rationale was abandoned under the Thatcher administration of the 1980s as public spending was expected to yield some measurable or economic return. The inherent validity of leisure provision as part of the public sector portfolio which had been accepted since the end of the previous century was replaced by a concept of leisure as a social investment and a tool for economic regeneration. Again, the potential of public libraries seems to have been overlooked in the majority of schemes established to achieve these ends. The competition and consumer-led demand which characterized the private sector were adopted as a model upon which public sector services were to operate. Many local authority services, among them the maintenance of grounds and parks and the management of leisure centres, were put out to tender, and some contracts were won by private sector organizations. There remains an implicit threat that contracting out may also be implemented in some aspects of the library service. There were serious suggestions of the (re)introduction of subscription lending departments, but the available evidence relating to those which were operated in the nineteenth century suggests that this would almost certainly result in a socially divisive library service which, in order to remain economically viable, would be forced to reflect primarily the demands of those able to pay, and thus to a two-tier form of leisure provision.

Leisure futures and the public library

Leisure is likely to become more, not less, important. Although the much vaunted leisure age shows no signs of immediate arrival, there is plenty of evidence to suggest that more people will have more leisure time, and that competition to provide for that leisure time will be intense. Earlier retirement and other changes in working patterns, together with demographic trends, are predicted to produce an older leisure market, with those in the 45–65 age bracket becoming increasingly important as a numerically dominant and economically powerful group. The relatively increasing affluence of some social groups will be attractive to private sector entrepreneurs, but of greater importance to the public sector will be economically and socially disadvantaged groups with limited leisure opportunities. Changes in life-style patterns, such as flexible working hours, working from home via computer link and short and fixed term contracts, are already having an impact upon 'traditional' leisure times such as evenings and weekends, and leisure providers will need to react accordingly; libraries may have to consider Sunday opening. The commercial leisure industry is likely to become more pervasive and ubiquitous. Whereas in the 1890s it produced cheap popular newspapers and novels, general chit-chat magazines and cinemas, the 1990s are experiencing the emergence of satellite and cable television on a global scale and technological advances in telecommunications and computer-based leisure which are contributing to the attraction of the home as a leisure environment. The ownership of the transnational media is concentrated in a powerful elite minority, and just as the commercial nature of the nineteenth-century booktrade encouraged the production of cheaper and more popular fiction, so the economic structures of media ownership are determining the nature of mass cultural production. The dichotomy between work and leisure which became more marked in the work ethic of the 1980s may be displaced by a more balanced approach in which consumerism wanes and quality of life assumes a greater importance. Conversely, continuing economic decline and social unrest would herald the return of a 'problem of leisure' and a more utilitarian rationale in which integration and control would be prominent.

The challenge to libraries is not to predict the precise nature of political, economic and social changes, but to develop a unified vision of their leisure function which will adapt to changing circumstances. Just as the first industrial revolution exercised a fundamental change in the modes of work, production and leisure, post-industrialization and the maturing of a post-industrial society will have an impact upon leisure values and the relationships between leisure and the quality of life. As Pat Coleman pointed out,[5] as work becomes less important and as full employment becomes a less likely reality, leisure becomes more important because it can provide the opportunities for personal development that were once provided by work and career. If public libraries can come to terms with this social change, they are well positioned to offer such opportunities.

While there are signs of a greater willingness to accept leisure, it is still not uncommon to hear senior librarians referring dismissively to the leisure uses of libraries as 'non-purposive' and by implication less important than other forms of use. There is little likelihood that progress in developing the library's leisure function will be made while this view persists. Librarians may need to consider in more detail the nature of the leisure uses of the public library and the extent to which they consider themselves as leisure managers and as equal partners in the formation of leisure policies at local and regional levels. The concept of leisure manager is possibly one with which many librarians might feel uncomfortable, but it is nevertheless an accurate reflection of the work in which many of them are engaged on a daily operational basis. There have already been some examples of innovative developments; Petersburn community library near Glasgow, for instance, responds to community leisure needs in lending not only books but compact discs and musical instruments and it also has a drop-in social centre for teenagers and a library-users' football team.[6] As the draft report of the Department of National Heritage's review of the public library service[7] showed, the role of the library as a community centre – providing a forum for meeting friends, being a familiar relaxing place – is valued by the public but not highly rated as often by librarians. A further possibility may be to develop library services which enable users to become creators as well as consumers of cultural production. This has already occurred in a small number of places where local writing groups have been based in libraries, but could be developed to offer people access to the means of producing their own newspapers and pamphlets, and sound or video recordings. Writers in residence in libraries are a familiar concept, but as libraries are involved in providing discs and tapes, musicians in residence might be an equally attractive method of encouraging creativity, particularly among younger people.

There would seem to be considerable benefits to the library profession in adopting a more leisure-orientated ideology, particularly in view of the rapid rate of change in public sector leisure provision and the emergence of a leisure management profession. The local government reorganization of 1974 contributed to a proliferation of managerial posts and professional activities, leading to the establishment of the Institute of Leisure and Amenity Management (ILAM) which embraces managers from all branches of the public, commercial and voluntary leisure sectors. Like The Library Association, ILAM has a structured membership to which admission can be gained only through an approved qualification scheme; again like The Library Association, it provides programmes of professional development and has a publishing programme. While both professional bodies have their own unique nature, they share many common aims and interests, and joint ventures between The Library Association and ILAM would promote the development of the library's leisure role. Librarians concerned about submergence in a world of leisure centres and fun pools would need have no fears in this respect, for in terms of outreach, customer care, the formation of regional and national networks and systems development they would have much from which leisure managers could learn. Not only would there be mutual benefit in cooperative ventures, but this would signify to the professional leisure community, and to the wider library community, a statement that libraries recognized themselves to have an integral role in the provision of leisure services.

At a local level, public libraries have many opportunities to develop their leisure function. The Library and Information Services Council recently published a model statement of how a public library might identify its leisure function in stating that:

> The library will develop and publicise its holdings of material in all formats to encourage the creative use of individuals' leisure time. It will assess and respond to the needs of people who use its services in their leisure time, whether for pleasure, information or education. It will recognise, in its stock and associated activities, that reading is a major form of recreation for many people.[8]

Welcome as this is, it is somewhat bland and could be refined. One metropolitan library authority in a leisure services department has a mission to work with the local community to '. . . maintain, develop and enhance the quality of life through the provision and encouragement of leisure opportunities', and this offers opportunities to think imaginatively about leisure in ways which do not necessarily have to be based upon book use. Staff working in this authority receive induction and training with employees in the leisure services department; library staff thus meet and are trained alongside sports, parks, museums, art gallery and theatre staff and are able to develop an awareness of the department's leisure ethos.

Public libraries also have many allies among novelists and celebrities in the arts world, though at a recent conference on the place of literature in libraries the discussion of the future relationships between these stalled on an assumption that literature and the arts were somehow incompatible with a library service based in a leisure department.[9] Libraries can work successfully with arts organizations, however, as a recent experiment in the promotion of fiction undertaken by Southern Arts in cooperation with Berkshire, Dorset and Hampshire library services shows.[10] There may also be a useful role in the support and promotion of first novels by new authors. However, although librarians appear to feel more at ease with programmes designed to promote literary fiction, it is important to remember that genre fiction is in greater demand, and, as a recent investigation noted, selection decisions relating to genre fictions are often undertaken with very little research or evidence of what readers derive from such books.[11]

Professional education and training

The final issue concerning the leisure development of public libraries is that of professional education and training. Undergraduate programmes are now dominated by information and methods of storing and accessing it electronically. Respective university prospectuses contain numerous references to information professions, information networks and pseudo-disciplines such as informatics. This is reasonable to the extent that the universities are training students for employment in establishments other than public libraries, but it is worth noting alongside this that several senior public library posts are given to people with skills in management and community responsiveness rather than with training and a career background in librarianship. The library profession in the nineteenth century complained that public libraries were not given serious recognition as part of the education system, and even as recently as the 1970s many librarians expressed the desire that their libraries should remain under the wing of an education department rather than move to a leisure department because of a belief that education was the true raison d'être of a public library. A similar state of affairs seems to be emerging now, in that the profession closely identifies itself with information, and promotes services by prefixing them with the word 'information'. As occurred in the past, the leisure function is of secondary importance, and the development of the vision and skills required to make libraries more relevant seems in danger of being left to other professions.

Leisure is important to everyone, and local authority leisure services are widely valued within their communities. Leisure managers and librarians have more aims in common than they have differences. Both are concerned to improve and enhance the quality of life, and have a high regard for the rights of the individual person. Both are community-orientated and have developed management and operational structures capable of responsiveness to community needs and wishes. Much recent development in local authority leisure provision has been in the area of community leisure in which services are not provider-led, but are managed in direct response to and in liaison with local people and community groups. The distinctions between libraries and leisure are to some extent being eroded, but the final and possibly the biggest obstacle to overcome is the reluctance to acknowledge that, in public libraries, most librarians are leisure managers as much as, if not more than, they are information managers.

NOTES AND REFERENCES TO CHAPTER 10

1   See: Henry, I., *The politics of leisure policy*, Macmillan, 1993, Chapters 1, 2 and 3, and Coalter, F., *Recreational welfare: the rationale for public sector leisure policy*, Avebury, 1988.

2   See, for examples of such projects: Great Britain, Department of the Environment, *Developing sport and leisure: good practice in urban regeneration*, HMSO, 1989.

3 Great Britain, House of Lords, *Sport and recreation*, HMSO, 1975.

4 See, for details: Library Advisory Council (England), *The libraries' choice*, HMSO, 1978.

5 Coleman, P., 'The changes and challenges facing library services', in Benington, J. and White, J. (eds.), *The future of leisure services*, Longman, 1988, 57–88.

6 Independent, 10 November 1994.

7 Department of National Heritage, *Review of the public library service in England and Wales, draft report September 1994, section 4: public library functions and services*, 10, Aslib.

8 Library and Information Services Council, *Setting objectives for public library services: a manual of public library objectives*, HMSO, 1991.

9 *Reading the future: a place for literature in public libraries*, Arts Council of Great Britain and Library Association Publishing, 1992.

10 *Well worth reading: an experiment in fiction promotion*, Direct Contact, 1990.

11 *Borrowed time?: the future of public libraries in the UK*, Comedia, 1993.

Appendix

THE FLOOD OF FICTION

A critic's complaint

The cry is still "They come! they come!"
Romances, novels, tales and stories,
Some treat of street, or slum and some
Of courtly scenes and regal glories.
More? more? – Well, well! a book's a book,
Sublime or simple, dull or clever,
And, like the Tennysonian brook,
Our book supply goes on forever;
No pause, no limit, no restriction,
One vast unending stream of Fiction.

Whence come they? Whither do they go?
And why are authors so prolific?
A million books a year, or so,
Four thousand novelists – terrific!
It stuns us, sweeps us off our feet,
Like whirling wind or raging torrent,
Light reading, once a pastime sweet,
Is now to me a task abhorrent;
No blessing, but a sore affliction,
This overwhelming mass of Fiction.

Like flowers that quickly bud and bloom,
Then droop and fade and fall to pieces,
Most novels meet an early doom,
Their glory in a season ceases;
Some seem like Dickens up-to-date,
While some are tinged with Scott or Lytton,
But, ah! so few are truly great,
We wonder why the rest were written;
Unmarked in subject, style or diction,
They form the rank and file of Fiction.

The volumed avalanche descends,
The motley printed pile grows higher,
Wherein the bulk of Fiction blends
With Truth— (itself too oft a liar) –
Adventures, travels, memoirs, "lives,"
With scandal their effect enhancing;
Munchausen's spirit still survives,
And much of history's mere romancing;
Thus even Truth, against conviction,
May swell the seething tide of Fiction.

Walter Parke

Published in *Library world* 1899-1900.

Index